Mosley's Blackshirts

The Inside Story of The British Union of Fascists 1932-1940

by
Jeffrey Hamm

Mosley's Blackshirts
The Inside Story of the British Union of Fascists
1932-1940

ISBN-13: 978-1-913176-14-3

Sanctuary Press Ltd
71-75 Shelton Street
Covent Garden
London
WC2H 9JQ

www.sanctuarypress.com
Email: info@sanctuarypress.com

Contents

Introduction

AFTER serving from October 1914 in the 16th Lancers and in Number 6 Squadron of the Royal Flying Corps, Oswald Ernald Mosley - acting on the suggestion of F. E. Smith (later Lord Birkenhead) - went into politics with two missions in mind: to create the promised "Land Fit for Heroes To Live In" and to prevent Britain becoming involved in another Great War. Mosley, the "political adventurer", followed these two objectives consistently throughout the remainder of his life.

He was elected Member of Parliament for Harrow in 1918 at the age of twenty-two, and for some time was the youngest Member.

In October 1920 Mosley crossed the floor in protest at the policy of reprisals in Ireland and became secretary of the Peace with Ireland Council.

By 1922, his cross-party position was worrying the Harrow Conservative and Unionist Association, and Mosley stood as an Independent in the General Election, winning by a majority of 7,422. In December of the following year Stanley Baldwin called a General Election, in which his Government was defeated. Mosley was again elected for Harrow, but with a reduced majority of 4,646. In his election speeches Mosley attacked the deflationary policy of the Cunliffe Committee as a main cause of unemployment.

The Conservative majority of 77 MP's was converted to a minority of 103; Labour gaining 191 seats, having won 142 the previous year. In January 1924, Ramsay MacDonald became the first Labour Prime Minister.

On 27th March, 1924 Mosley applied for membership of the Labour Party and received a warm letter of welcome from MacDonald expressing the hope that he would find therein "a wide field in which you can show your usefulness."

In April Mosley delivered a speech to the Independent Labour Party Conference. He got on well with Jimmy Maxton, then MP for Bridgeton and later I.L.P. Chairman but was regarded with intense dislike by Herbert Morrison and Hugh Dalton. (Maxton, who had been imprisoned in the First War, later visited Mosley when he too was imprisoned; one of the few politicians to do so).

As a valued new recruit, Mosley received many offers of seats, including Ladywood, Birmingham, where Neville Chamberlain was the sitting Member. The idea of defeating a member of the Chamberlain dynasty, which had ruled Birmingham for sixty years as Liberal-Radicals and later as Conservative-Unionists appealed strongly to Mosley. He was adopted unanimously. The campaign was going splendidly until the Zinoviev Letter was published and induced many Liberal-minded voters to switch hastily from Labour to Tory. Even so, Neville Chamberlain only scraped back, after two recounts, with a seventy-seven majority.

Out of Parliament by a narrow margin, Mosley devoted the next two years to travel and political thinking. He visited India and America, where he met Roosevelt. In May 1924 he had inspected the slums of Liverpool and had been appalled by what he saw. Such poverty, he reasoned, was caused only by lack of effective demand, because the necessary resources - men and machines - existed to abolish it. He decided to devote himself to the economic problem of poverty and unemployment, which led to his first great economic plan - the Birmingham Proposals, detailed in a speech at the I.L.P. Summer School in August 1925.

These proposals were the result of Mosley's many discussions with Keynes, the economists of the American Federal Reserve Board and the American technocrats.

There was a conflict of interest between workers and manufacturers and rentiers and bankers. Finance was the enemy of producers. Total demand should be increased by issuing consumers' credits to the unemployed and producers' credits to manufacturers. There would be no danger of inflation until unemployment had declined to a point at which the maximum production of the nation had been reached.

Mosley's Plan, put to a delegate meeting of the Birmingham Labour Party was later published under the title of *Revolution By Reason*. Demand must be expanded, because deflation had reduced it below the level necessary to achieve full employment. The credit expansion had to be planned, because it was essential that the poor received the new money. An Economic Planning Council would decide the flow of credit. Production would be switched to the home market and all necessary foods and raw materials purchased by far fewer exports.

In December 1926 Mosley contested the by-election at Smethwick. Despite a particularly vicious press campaign against "the rich Socialists" he won with a majority of 6,582.

Winston Churchill - to his own great surprise and that of everyone else - had been offered the Chancellorship of the Exchequer by Baldwin after the 1924 General Election. With his minuscule knowledge of the nation's finances, Churchill relied entirely on the advice he received from the Treasury, the Bank of England and the City of London.

When Churchill put Britain back on the Gold Standard at the pre-1914 exchange rate Mosley warned that it would mean wage reductions and higher unemployment. On the day that Churchill announced in his first budget that the Bank of England was to sell gold in support of an exchange rate of $4.86 to the pound, *The Times* published a letter from Mosley in which he protested at "an unnaturally high rate of exchange artificially maintained in the chimerical pursuit of the dollar." Mosley's line of argument was fully supported by Keynes, who expanded it into a book *The Economic Consequences of Mr. Churchill.*

One direct consequence of returning to the Gold Standard was the 1926 General Strike. To sell abroad, prices had to be cut, because British exports had become much more costly, and the only way prices could be cut was by reducing wages. The industry hardest hit was coal mining. On 30th April, 1926 the owners announced that they could only employ the miners at a lower wage. The miners struck, and although the General Strike called by the TUC only lasted for nine days, the miners held out for another six months.

Mosley had joined the Independent Labour Party as well as the Labour Party - membership of both being permitted - and in 1927 he was elected to the ILP's National Administrative Council. He remained on it for two years.

Mosley was also the first politician to warn that protective tariffs could be circumvented by deliberate devaluation. Forty years later, devaluing currencies to boost exports had become common practice - and a major world problem. The ILP had been established in 1893, under the leadership of Keir Hardie, to secure Labour and Socialist seats in Parliament and by the 1920s had become an influential ginger group within, but on the Left of the Labour Party.

In the 1929 General Election, in which Labour became the largest Parliamentary party, with 287 seats, Mosley was returned for Smethwick with a majority of 7,340. Dependent on Liberal neutrality, the Labour Government found it difficult to legislate. Ramsay MacDonald appointed Mosley Chancellor of the Duchy of Lancaster, with special responsibility for the unemployment problem, reporting to the totally incompetent Lord Privy Seal and Employment Minister, J. H Thomas.

Each week Mosley and J. H. Thomas met all the top Civil

Servants to review the employment situation. After it became clear that Thomas had no idea what the others were talking about ("I ain't understood a bloody word") Mosley saw as little of Thomas as possible. Instead he got on with the task of working out a detailed policy for dealing with unemployment.

Remarks in a ministerial report on pensions drafted by Mosley for submission to the Cabinet are apposite: "A man of 60 who has worked all his life will not suffer much demoralisation through living in idleness, but a man of 20 may suffer irreparable harm. By keeping the young in idleness we destroy the human material upon which the future prosperity of reconstructed industry must be built . . . Idleness may be a boon to the old, but it is a damnation to the young."

The Cabinet rejected the plan. Mosley soon discovered that the Labour Government was only willing to spend money to make industry more competitive for the benefit of the export trade - not just to provide work.

After getting Keynes' approval of his proposals for dealing with unemployment, Mosley sent a copy to Thomas and the Cabinet. The first section of the Mosley Memorandum dealt with the machinery of government; the second, long-term reconstruction; the third, short-term emergency measures; and the fourth, monetary policy. Basically, Mosley was proposing an executive committee led by the Prime Minister, consisting of ministers responsible for economic policy, advised by top economists and scientists and with a secretariat of 12 higher civil servants.

When the Memorandum was discussed at the Cabinet and ministerial meetings on 13th and 19th May, 1930 Mosley met with blank incomprehension from his colleagues. The next day he resigned office.

In the debate on unemployment on 28th May, Mosley spoke for more than an hour. When he sat down he received one of the greatest ovations in Parliamentary history. Writing of this event nearly 40 years later, Mosley said: "When I resigned from the Government, in effect I staked my whole political life on two main issues. The first was that this top-heavy island cannot continue indefinitely to sell so large a proportion of its total production on the open markets of the world . . . The second was that the purchasing power of the Western world could not indefinitely absorb the production of modern science without the devising by government of new economic policies of a totally different order to the ideas then prevailing . . ." - My Life

At the Labour Party Conference at Llandudno on 6th October, 1930 a resolution from Doncaster called for an N.E.C. report on the Mosley Memorandum and Mosley put his case to the assembled delegates. The resolution was narrowly defeated, and only by the union block votes - 1,046,000 for, 1,251,000 against.

On 8th December, 1930, Mosley published a definite statement of policy, the Mosley Manifesto in the *Daily Telegraph*. It proposed an emergency Cabinet of not more than five Ministers to see through a plan to develop new industries and modernise existing ones. The home market would be the basis of British trade. The slums would be replaced with new homes, thus providing work for many of the unemployed. Seventeen MPs and the General Secretary of the Miners' Federation signed it.

In January 1931, William Morris (later Lord Nuffield) handed Mosley a cheque for £50,000 to form a new party. In February Mosley went ahead, and the New Party was launched on 1st March 1931. It was ill-fated from the very beginning. Mosley himself fell ill with pleurisy and pneumonia. Its meetings were invariably disrupted by Labourites and communists. Even so, it secured important recruits: Harold Nicolson, Professor C. E. M. Joad, the Sitwells and Peter Howard.

Six weeks after it was founded, the New Party contested a by-election at Ashton-under-Lyne and gained a respectable 4,472 votes.

Labour supporters were furious at Mosley "letting the Tories in" (they would direct equal fury at the SDP in the 1980s) and many of the New Party's subsequent meetings were turned into chaos by them. As the New Party depended almost entirely on meetings to put its case, a force of stewards was organised to keep order at its meetings.

The New Party put up 24 candidates in the October General Election. All these candidates, except Mosley at Stoke - where he polled 10,534 votes - and Sellick Davies at Merthyr, lost their deposits, with an average of 1,036 votes each.

In the emergency caused by a flight from the pound, MacDonald and Baldwin called for a "doctor's mandate" to overcome the crisis, and won a landslide victory for their National Government.

Mosley decided that he had to reform his organisation to meet an entirely new situation. After visiting Italy with Harold Nicolson and others, and meeting Mussolini, Mosley announced his decision to close the New Party on 5th April 1932. He would found a New Movement, a union of the best and most vital elements of the nation, and would call it the British Union of Fascists.

Thus it was that Mosley's book The Greater Britain saw publication on 1st October, 1932, and two days later the BUF was launched on its short and stormy existence at a ceremony at the former New Party offices in Great George Street, Westminster attended by 32 founder-members.

Mosley's original intellectual associates - the "talkers" - were soon replaced by the "doers" - ordinary "men and women with the vision to see the doom coming to the values and position of their country and with the will and courage to resist it."

Within eighteen months - by the Spring of 1934 - twenty thousand such men and women had donned the black shirt.

"We ask those who join us to march with us in a great and hazardous adventure. We ask them to be prepared to sacrifice all, but to do so for no small and unworthy ends. We can only offer them the deep belief that they are fighting that a great land may live." - Oswald Mosley, 1st October, 1932

The flavour of a thousand Mosley speeches was captured by the *Manchester Guardian* reporter who wrote :

He begins very smilingly with some references to his legend, but he has not got very far before the smile disappears and the face says clearly "into battle". It is an earnest, gripping mood. First that apathetic audience is arrested, then stirred, and finally . . . swept off its feet by a tornado of a peroration yelled at the defiant high pitch of a tremendous voice - a peroration denouncing the old men "who muddled my generation into the crisis of 1914 . . . who have laid waste the power and glory of our land . . . from whose tired old hands, stained with blood and disasters innumerable, our flag is slipping down into dust and dishonour".

Jeffrey Hamm

The East London Shopkeeper

IN THE SPRING of 1983, three former Blackshirts, all from the North of England, appeared on a Television programme. None of them regretted his political past. Each expressed his continuing loyalty to Mosley. What kind of movement and what kind of man could have inspired such devotion? To attempt an answer I must go back to Christmas Eve 1933, when a schoolboy was taken by his Mother as a Christmas treat to see the decorations and displays in the West End of London. Near the entrance to Piccadilly Circus Underground at the lower end of Regent Street stood a man dressed in a black shirt and grey trousers. He was selling a newspaper. I bought a copy of *The Fascist Week* and read it on the way home. I liked the idea of a movement whose aim was "national revival", so, my interest aroused, I borrowed a copy of Mosley's book *The Greater Britain* from the public library.

Some weeks later I came across another Blackshirt, who was selling this paper in Leytonstone High Street. I eagerly bought a copy.

This man, whose name was Richardson, was typical of those who supported the BUF from its beginning, and deserves to be mentioned. Pinned proudly to his chest were the four brightly polished medals he had won in the First World War - a war that had left 750,000 Britons dead and 1½ million maimed.

Strangely enough, Richardson always seemed to be crying. Tears rolled continuously down his face and he wiped them constantly with a handkerchief. Richardson had been gassed in the Somme battles in 1916. He was one of more than 1¼ million gas casualties. After his discharge from the Army he had existed on a disability pension of about 10 shillings a week. With a respiratory system half-destroyed by poison gas, Richardson did not live to see the outbreak of another war.

In general terms, those who joined the BUF believed in Christianity, the Monarchy, the British Empire and in saving Europe from the menace of Communism. But the BUF had a detailed economic policy which would make sense today.

A political party is seldom if ever supported for the reasons it is opposed. Like many I was very attracted by a vigorous radical programme calling for an occupational franchise, military preparedness, the revival of British agriculture - then in a parlous state - and a huge public works scheme which would systematically wipe out the slums and provide work for the unemployed. This programme had been worked out in consultation with the leading economist of the age, Professor John Maynard Keynes, by a rich man who as a Member of Parliament and a Government Minister had tried in vain for a dozen years to get the "old gang" politicians to provide his ex-service comrades with work and hope, and who cared passionately about the plight of the poor.

In his resignation speech on 28 May 1930 Mosley said:

"This nation has to be mobilised and rallied for a tremendous effort, and who can do that except the Government of the day? If that effort is not made we may soon come to a crisis, to a real crisis. I do not fear that so much, for this reason, that in a crisis this nation is always at its best. This people knows how to handle a crisis, it cools their heads and steels their nerves. What I fear much more than a sudden crisis is a long, slow crumbling through the years ... a gradual paralysis beneath which all the vigour and energy of this country will succumb. That is a far more dangerous thing, and far more likely to happen unless some effort is made."

I always thought of the BUF as being a movement of the Right, though many of the finest people in it were former Socialists and Communists. The present-day political label of "Radical Right" suits the BUF quite well. My own description of us would be: "Traditionalists who advocated a root-and-branch reform of the economic system". We were economic revolutionaries rather than political ones.

In the early 1930s the paradox of "poverty in the midst of plenty" troubled the minds of a great many people. The newspapers were full of stories of Canadian farmers burning their wheat, of Brazilians burning their coffee and of British trawlermen throwing their catches of cod and herring back into the sea because there were no buyers - and all this at a time of widespread deprivation and malnutrition. So we all asked the question: why had production outgrown consumption? What was wrong with distribution? with the economic system?

Apart from the Marxists with their own idée fixe there were those like the engineer Major C. H. Douglas who argued that there was an inherent deficiency, a permanent gap between the quantity of money distributed in wage-form in the course of industrial production and the retail prices of the goods produced. Others believed that all the misery was due to Montagu Norman's attempt as Governor of the Bank of England to return to the gold standard at pre-1914 parity regardless of the money shortage and consequent unemployment this policy caused.

In the United States similar searching questions were being asked by Columbia University professors and Federal Reserve Board officials who called themselves "Technocrats" - a term that, thanks to the new problems introduced by the Computer Age, is rapidly coming back into use. The American technocrats reasoned that our modern industrial society was becoming far too complex to be run by politicians and should be controlled by engineers and scientists.

Just before reading E. G. Mandeville Roe's *The Corporate State* I had learned of the technocratic viewpoint from an American book entitled *An Introduction to Technocracy*. A system of government in which Parliament was elected not by geographical constituencies but by professional, industrial and trade corporations which included both employers and employees seemed to me to be the ideal way to put the ideas of the American Technocrats into practice and solve the awesome problems caused by the growing replacement of man by machine.

I joined the BUF after carefully reading its literature for months, but not without difficulty.

From the Spring of 1934, the Movement had expanded rapidly, aided by the enthusiastic support of Lord Rothermere's newspapers *The Daily Mail* and *The Evening News*. At school we were already divided into Communists and Fascists. I remember one of my group playing truant one day and when we asked him where he had been he said: to the BUF Headquarters at 33 King's Road, Chelsea and had seen Mosley. We were greatly impressed.

Walking down Fairlop Road, Leytonstone one day I was surprised and delighted to see that a BUF branch had opened there. I took to calling in every day after school, until I was told by the branch organiser that he didn't want schoolboys hanging around! This was Hector McKechnie, who had been the British Consul in the Central American state of Honduras. Shortly after, he moved to National Headquarters, there to handle more important matters.

After the Young Conservatives in Leyton joined the BUF en masse the branch moved to larger premises in Leytonstone High Road. A typical BUF branch was situated over a shop and consisted of two rooms: one an office for the branch officials - the organiser, treasurer, women's organiser, propaganda officer, etc., and a larger room where tea and light refreshments could be served from, a small bar, and members' meetings held.

I submitted an application for membership, but being under age had to go to NHQ to be interviewed by Captain B. D. E. Donovan, an ex-Indian Army officer who was third in command. After questioning me at length and satisfying himself that I understood the BUF's policy he gave me special permission to join.

Outdoor meetings of Leytonstone Branch were held on Friday evenings outside a public house. A van would arrive from NHQ bearing the speaker, who was often a well-spoken man named Montgomery and who sported a monocle, plus five or six stewards who formed a half-circle round the speaker to protect him should the Red Front decide to rush the platform instead of merely jeering and heckling. How the sight of the monocled Montgomery must have infuriated them!

In the 1920s and 1930s the only people in Britain who enjoyed free speech were the Socialists and Communists, who regularly and systematically broke up the meetings of Tories and anyone else they disliked. They broke up Mosley's meetings even before he founded the BUF.

I first saw Mosley and heard him speak when he addressed an audience of ten thousand at the Albert Hall, on Sunday, 22 April 1934. This meeting was entirely peaceful and very enthusiastic. He made a dramatic entrance, to the strains of a march, Mosley!, specially composed for the occasion by Lord Berners.

I did not go to the much-criticized meeting at Olympia in June. What happened there was this: an army of Communists carrying knuckledusters, coshes and iron bars tried to smash the meeting and were met head on by our stewards who threw them out. Unfortunately a few innocents trapped in the middle were also thrown out.

The Leftwing intellectuals - Burgess and Philby among them perhaps? - who received black eyes and bruises set up such a howl afterwards one would have thought that a second Massacre at Amritsar or Peterloo had taken place. But no-one had been killed or even seriously injured - a miracle considering the fearsome weapons carried by the Reds - though a good many people, including many Blackshirts, needed hospital treatment.

The events at Olympia are aptly summed up by an old French proverb: Cet animal est tres mechant; quand on l'attaque, il se defend. Because we defended our meetings from orchestrated attack we were called thugs. You certainly needed to be tough of body and resolute in spirit to stay in the BUF. Many a young Blackshirt was forced to leave home by an irate Conservative or Socialist father; lost his job because of his politics; was beaten up by "car-cruising" opponents when he stood on the street selling our newspapers.

From the day I joined in October 1934 practically all my time in the evenings and at the weekends was devoted to the BUF. There were outdoor meetings to support and sales drives to take part in. On Saturday mornings copies of *The Blackshirt* had to be delivered to the homes of subscribers.

On Saturday evenings in the High Streets of Britain, a dozen or more men and women would stand selling political newspapers - *The Blackshirt, Daily Worker, New Leader* - Fascists, Communists, ILPers, and Social Crediters all trying to shout down the others.

By 1935, the BUF had some 600 branches and sub-branches, mostly in England but with a few in Wales and Scotland. I doubt if we had much support in Glasgow, but the branch organizer there, Stewart-Hunter, a crippled ex-Serviceman, was frequently beaten up by Communists. We must have had a substantial number of members somewhere in Scotland - Edinburgh perhaps? - because on a visit to NHQ I saw a large contingent of Scotsmen in kilts - and black shirts!

There was always plenty of humour in the BUF, and we could take a joke against ourselves. I liked the story of the Blackshirt speaker in Tottenham who was persistently heckled by a Red with the cry of "What abaht Olympia?"

"Well, what abaht Olympia?" asked the speaker sarcastically.

"What abaht the bloke wot got thrown down four bleeding flight of stairs, 'ad the bleeding trousers torn off 'is arse, and then got arrested by the police for disorderly conduct?"

"You can't believe the lies you read in the newspapers", replied the speaker.

"Newspapers be buggered!" came the reply. "I WOZ THE BLOKE!"

I became an organizer for the BUF's Youth Movement, which involved visiting branches in many parts of North and East London - in Bethnal Green, Shoreditch, Hackney, Stoke Newington, Poplar, Limehouse, Enfield, Walthamstow, Chingford, Leyton, Forest Gate, East Ham, Ilford, and as far afield as Southend. In some of these places the BUF had several branches.

On moving to Loughton in 1938 I transferred to the Epping Branch. This was "Churchill territory" but this branch with its headquarters in South Woodford was a large and flourishing one with more than 200 members, some of them very interesting people, such as Major Fitzgerald, who had been military attaché at the British Embassy in Paris.

In the spring of 1939, with the help of a loan from my father, I acquired a retail shop in West Ham, and transferred back to the reopened Leytonstone Branch.

Mosley believed in a well-armed Britain and encouraged his supporters to join the Territorials and the Royal Air Force. (No doubt the twits then in charge of British Intelligence thought this very sinister.) The BUF stressed the importance of air power and numbered among its supporters the aviation pioneer, Sir Alliott Verdon Roe, who had been the very first Englishman to fly, and who designed the Avro aircraft. The editor of *The Aeroplane* was a sympathizer, while that journal's sub-editor, Geoffrey Dorman, who had flown with Mosley in the Royal Flying Corps, was a BUF member and became editor of our newspaper, Action. Members of the BUF also belonged to the Air League of the British Empire, the Secretary of which, Colonel Norman Thwaites, was also Chairman of the BUF's January Club.

When on the outbreak of the Second World War all these Blackshirt reservists were called up, the BUF lost the services of many of its most ardent members, including more than 300 of its branch organizers.

Several of my school friends had joined the RAF at the time of its expansion in 1936, when the RAF Volunteer Reserve was also established. From the autumn of 1939, I heard of the death of someone I knew, every few months.

Something else happened on 3 September 1939. The father of our Branch organizer in Leytonstone had been killed in the First World War. Our Branch organizer's mother and grandmother could not face the ordeal of another war: they committed suicide.

In the spring of 1940, the RAF - to which I devote particular attention because it is the Force in which I served for more than four years - suffered appalling losses in its bombing raids on German warships (it was no "Phoney War" in the air!) and could ill-afford to lose any of its experienced Blackshirt aircrew, some of whom had flown with Mosley 22 years earlier. But in the Great Invasion Panic which followed the Fall of France and the "small boat" evacuation of Dunkirk - in which at least three Blackshirts, C. P. Dick, Eric Hamilton Piercy and D. Merriman - made trips in their boats to rescue British soldiers, some of our RAF members were arrested, among them Squadron Leader Thomson of Barnet

Branch. Others could not be arrested: they had died on 19 March, taking part in the very first attack by Bomber Command on a German land target - the seaplane base on the Island of Sylt.

How our highest-ranking supporter in the Royal Air Force escaped the dragnet remains a mystery to this day. Air Commodore Sir J. A. Chamier, who had been Secretary-General of the Air League of the British Empire and a member of the BUF's influential January Club, was also suspected by the Government of being one of our most generous financial backers. It seems inconceivable that he was left alone through sheer blundering incompetence on the part of MI5 A senior officer who had been Technical Director of Vickers and Director of Technical Development at the Air Ministry was probably as near to being indispensable as any man could be in the nation's circumstances at the time. Like hundreds of other BUF members and supporters in the RAF he received not detention but rapid promotion - he was made Commandant of the Air Training Corps and later wrote the official history of the RAF.

On 23 May 1940, Mosley and 32 of the Headquarters staff were arrested. During the succeeding weeks 800 other members were also arrested, including all the Movement's Parliamentary candidates. These arrests were carried out in such a haphazard way that I have never had any faith in the Intelligence Services since - a scepticism amply justified by the Government's embarrassed admission that the Intelligence agent appointed in 1940 to trap "spies and traitors" was - Anthony Blunt.

The BUF's membership was divided into two categories: Active and Non-Active. Numerous non-active members found themselves in jail while some of the most active ones were left untroubled throughout the war. I have often puzzled about this since, and have reached the conclusion that it all depended on whether or not one's name had appeared in one of our publications. So a farmer who had written a letter to *Action* complaining about tithes or a would-be tenant who had advertised for a flat . . .

The internment for months and years in Britain's prisons and concentration camps of some of the superpatriots of the BUF is another story. As for its justification I will quote the judgment of a distinguished historian. In *The Observer* on 30 October 1983, Professor A. J. P. Taylor wrote: "The Home Secretary had no foundation for suspicion against Mosley and never found any."

More than half a century has now passed. How do I feel, looking back on these events?

It cannot be stressed too strongly or too often that Fascism was never an international conspiracy directed from a single centre as Communism was and is. Mosley may have borrowed Italian and German trappings but the BUF was a highly patriotic, law-abiding movement with a serious policy for solving Britain's problems.

I would say that during the eight years of its existence, the BUF represented the political viewpoint of a quarter of a million or more British people, many of whom joined it, if only for a short period. At any given time, it had 30,000 members, of whom 10,000 were activists. Many of those whose membership lapsed remained sympathetic to us.

Like those three Northerners who appeared on television, I make no apologies for having belonged to a movement dedicated to national renaissance, supported by thousands of decent, patriotic British men and women. I am grateful for having had the privilege of meeting so many fine and wonderful people in it - many of whom would shortly die in a war they deplored.

The consequences of that fateful decision to destroy Nazi Germany are with us, and the freedom and democracy that Britain went to war to preserve have disappeared from half of Europe and two-thirds of the world. Mankind faces two horrific prospects: nuclear annihilation or Soviet Communist slavery.

Whenever I reflect on the BUF's unhappy and unjust end, and, more particularly, what has happened to England since, I recall Mosley's inspiring and prophetic words at our Movement's beginning:

"Better the great adventure, better the great attempt for England's sake, better defeat, disaster, better far the end of that trivial thing called a political career, than stilling in a uniform of blue and gold, strutting and posturing on the stage of little England, amid the scenery of decadence, until history, in turning over an heroic page of the human story, writes of us the contemptuous postscript: 'These were the men to whom was entrusted the Empire of Great Britain, and whose idleness, ignorance and cowardice left it no better than Spain.' We shall win; or at least we shall return upon our shields."

Had the British public paid attention to what Mosley was saying in the 1930s, the whole course of history would have been different. Britain would have remained a Great Power with its Empire intact, and 25 million Europeans would not have lost their lives in a final, futile attempt to preserve the 'balance of power'.

Leonard Wise

The Suffolk Landowner

MY FAMILY, originating in a lordship between Dieppe and Rouen, held extensive lands in Norfolk from the beginning of the 13th century and right up to 1931 had an interest in more than 80 farms in Norfolk and Suffolk.

Until his death on 19 May 1954 my father lived at Monk Soham Hall, Woodbridge, Suffolk. He liked his walks in the early morning. From my bedroom window I would watch his lone figure in the distance, appearing and disappearing over the inclines and declines of the property. Sometimes I would go out to meet him and we would converse at length on politics, ethnology and general philosophy. My father encouraged me from an early age to take responsibility, enjoy sporting activities and adopt an individual and independent attitude. Thus I frequently went off to London and other great cities to seek the company and learn from the erudite and enlightened. During the day I spent my time with some social coterie and at night I visited the destitute and deprived remnants of society. Associating with the "Two Nations" enabled me to gain a balanced judgment in the distressful days of the Thirties. Wealth and poverty; ostentation and deprivation. Much that I saw alarmed and distressed me: the heedless vulgarity on the one side and the sordidness on the other. Inequality there must be, but this was pitiless inequality.

In contrast with the festering cities, the countryside was at least clean, its poverty bearable. The lot of landowners and farmers had been a testing struggle even before the First World War. All around land fell into neglect and farmsteads into a shambles of decay. In 1933, my father was offered virtually the whole of a village which the Church Commissioners had seized as a tithe debt, on condition that he paid the arrears which had been owing for some five years. My father could well have done so but he refused and no-one else would accept the bait. The land lay dormant up to the outbreak of war in 1939; overgrown with weeds it was a scene of utter desolation. Many farmers over a wide, surrounding area were in debt to my father and I would drive him round to visit them. His sympathetic generosity, extended at considerable financial loss to himself, enabled some of them to survive to better days.

Up to the age of 21 I was fully occupied with work, sport and study. Philosophy attracted me more than history, which I considered one-sided and unreasoning. I conceived my own philosophy as Darwinian pantheism. The aim of one's transient life, I decided, should be to give more than one takes.

In 1930 I took over the full occupation, responsibility for and use of Cranley Manor, on the outskirts of the small Borough town of Eye. Later I inherited this property. As a man who was never less alone than when alone, this arrangement suited me splendidly. My reading and studying could continue without interruption, while my personal household wants were provided by a thoughtful housekeeper and her husband, to both of whom I have ever since been indebted. I married in 1933. My capable and gifted wife has shared with fortitude and understanding the long struggle for our beliefs and aims.

Social life with its At Homes, leaving of visiting cards, and stultifying gatherings was never my forte. I regarded the social round as empty, shallow, backbiting and insular. Though a member of an old-established, traditional Conservative family I felt that the Conservative Party had conserved only for a privileged few and that its policies had reduced the majority of our people to misery and poverty.

For several years I read, pondered and observed, and expressed my views in contentious letters to the Press. In response to one of these letters I one day received a parcel containing some of Sir Oswald Mosley's writings, and literature explaining the policies of his Movement. After two months' deliberation I decided that Mosley was right and that henceforth I would join his Movement and work for its cause.

It was obvious to me that British agriculture and industry were being sacrificed for the sole benefit of international financiers who reaped a higher rate of interest on their investments in low-paid, sweated countries and that in consequence cheap food and manufactures flooded into Britain, to the detriment of our industries and workers. This financial trickery was being exposed by a selfless, fearless man of outstanding intellectual gifts and total sincerity. This man was no posturing demagogue but a far-sighted patriot.

The local BUF branch organiser arranged a personal interview with Mosley, at my request, and travelled up to London with me. When I entered Mosley's office he rose and we shook hands firmly. We looked at each other straight, and I immediately felt that there was a complete mutual understanding between us that required no words to express. On that same day, I had tea with another leading member of considerable character and ability - A. Raven Thomson.

Soon I was responsible for my own branch, in the Eye Parliamentary District. With the aid of strong-minded and reliable deputy leaders we held regular meetings, selling our newspapers on the streets and delivering them to remote country houses. Communists from nearby Leiston came over to heckle and attack us, and when I attended London meetings it was noticeable that it was the Communists who organised the violence.

In 1938 I stood for election to the Eye Borough Council as local leader of the BUF. Though I had undertaken little canvassing I was voted on to the Council, made my speech on the Town Hall steps, and attended the Council's meetings thereafter. Shortly after my election, I received a letter from Mosley in which he said: "I write to congratulate you very warmly on your success and to thank you for the signal service you have performed for the Movement by your fight".

At a Council meeting, with opposition from only one Councillor, I succeeded in securing the Eye Town Hall for a meeting to be addressed by Mosley. On the day of the meeting I arranged for loudspeakers to be attached to the four outside walls of the Town Hall, so that Mosley's speech could be relayed to an outside audience and heard by most people in the Borough.

Sir Oswald and his party arrived at my house at about 6.30 p.m. to dine with my wife and myself before proceeding to the meeting, which was due to start at 8 p.m. At 7.45 p.m. we went for a short stroll across my lawns and around my garden and became engrossed in a discussion on philosophy and philosophers, on country lore and kindred subjects. Deeply immersed, we suddenly heard the Town Hall clock strike 8 p.m. a mile away in the valley.

Mosley had never been known to be late for a meeting. We hastily jumped into a car and arrived at the Town Hall a minute or two late, entering by a side door. Outside, the square and streets were crowded, some imported Communists waited, obviously intent on creating a disturbance. Inside, the Hall was packed with a well-mannered audience who listened attentively to Sir Oswald's speech. After Mosley had finished, I made a brief speech against the din made by the Communist opposition outside and the stones and brickbats thrown by them at the back wall behind the speakers' platform.

Returning to my house that night, I arranged a private meeting of my members, who had been heartened by the enthusiasm shown at the Town Hall meeting. As well as increased support after Mosley's appearance in Eye we met with increased opposition. This I found encouraging. We held more public and private meetings and sold our newspapers in the streets of Norwich, Ipswich and the towns and villages of my Parliamentary area. Our membership increased week by week, even though I would accept only the best and most trustworthy applicants, for I regarded the recruitment of persons of character, courage and reliability as being essential to the success of our struggle.

By 1939, it was clear that a great many people were beginning to rebel against the hopelessness and decay of the old political order. In the countryside, first-class medium-loam farms could be bought for less than £4 an acre, while in the towns whole industries were collapsing under the competition of cheap imported goods.

Contrary to popular mythology, in the late 1930s the British people were turning to Mosley and his policy of economic sanity in rapidly growing numbers. Then came an unnecessary war which lay waste the whole of Europe and cost millions of lives. Britain could have got an accommodation with the "Have-Not" Powers which would have made Europe and its overseas territories invulnerable, self-sustaining and subservient to neither Russia nor America.

For nine months after Britain's ridiculous and worthless Guarantee to Poland and declaration of war, we of the BUF continued to advocate an honourable, negotiated peace. Then in the late Spring of 1940 the infamous Regulation 18B was used to silence us. Hundreds of true patriots were seized in their homes and at their workplaces and thrown into prison without charge or trial.

There we were treated worse than convicted criminals and subjected to every indignity and degradation. Many of us who were confined in Walton Jail, Liverpool spent 23½ hours a day in solitary confinement, being allowed only half-an-hour's exercise a day in the prison courtyard. Compelled to walk apart, we were not allowed to speak to one another. The only sound was the tramping of feet and an occasional warning shout from a warder if he detected a whispered voice. Nightly the Luftwaffe bombed the Liverpool docks and one night there was a direct hit on the prison.

In due course we were moved to concentration camps, such as the one at Ascot. Here, a heavy, double barbed-wire enclosure was flanked by machine-gun turrets, and revolver-and-rifle-equipped guards patrolled the perimeter night and day. It was both pathetic and amusing, but nevertheless part of an enormous tragedy - the needless self-destruction of the West.

The concentration camps provided us with some relief - we could mix and converse with the colourful melange of detainees from all walks of life. Some had arrived from Brixton Prison where Mosley was held, and it strengthened our hearts to learn that he was well and undaunted in spirit. Our contingent from Walton contained Catholic priests and Protestant clergymen, well-known authors, university dons, large estate owners, farmers, farm workers, doctors, accountants, retired pensioners in the seventies, and naval, air force and army officers, some still in uniform. All had been torn from their homes, wives, children, employees and places of work without being able to arrange for their dependants' security or welfare. Empty homes and shops were robbed. For many it was a calamity from which they never recovered.

Eventually I appeared before the Government's secret tribunal. My inquisitors asked me what I had meant in a public declaration at the time Britain declared war that "all was lost". What was indeed lost to Britain, Europe and the West was far greater than any of us could possibly have imagined at that time.

After my release from Ascot concentration camp, armed guards accompanied me to Ascot Railway Station. I was given a warrant to take me home. My identity card was returned to me endorsed in red to the effect that I was forbidden to move more than five miles from my home without the permission of the Chief Constable of Suffolk. A letter signed by the Secretary of State confirmed this. What an insult and farce it all was!

Fortunately for me my local police and Chief Constable were understanding. They allowed me some elasticity and I owe them much gratitude.

After the war ended, when Churchill stole from Mosley his idea of a United Europe, I received a letter signed by Churchill asking me to give him my backing! I wrote to him saying that he now expected us to support that which he had done more than anyone to destroy.

In my heavily-locked prison cell, 6 feet by 12, in which the days were measured only by alternating light and dark, I philosophised ruefully on the mysterious nature of man and the devious ways in which he enacts his laws. We of the BUF said and did what we believed to be right, and I am sure that in time truth will expose the falsity that denounced us. Indeed the process of historical correction and rethinking has already begun.

In my study, piled high with books, many written by old and valued friends, is one of my proudest possessions: a large, framed photograph of Sir Oswald Mosley on which he had written, on 11 November 1965: "To my old friend and companion Ronald Creasy from Mosley".

Serious-minded people frequently ask me: "How did Mosley feel in the last years of his life?" I can only answer that his mind was completely at peace. Jonathan Swift, compelled to go into exile to Dublin to escape his political enemies once wrote:

"When a true genius appears in the world you may know him by this sign, that all the dunces are in confederacy against him".

Mosley could afford a tranquil mind: he had taken no part in the destruction of Britain and Europe. Unlike Swift, Mosley went into exile voluntarily, to "help make Europe", for he felt that it was still possible for Britain to recapture some of its old glory as an equal partner in a great new European Nation, a Power capable of withstanding all outside threats. To his last hour, Mosley remained centuries ahead of the jealous and spiteful "dunces" who oppressed him and denigrated his noble vision and his burning patriotism. Shortly before his death I met him for the last time at a gathering in London. No matter that our conversation was brief. He had others to see and greet. We clasped hands warmly and our eyes met in the same totality of understanding that we had experienced so many years before. In my heart there was deep sorrow, for I felt the chiming of the hour. We had written to one another about Oswald Spengler's philosophy, with which Mosley at first disagreed but later largely accepted. The 'hour of decision' was clearly approaching for this man of supreme distinction and undying spirit. Those of us who followed him may well feel that we too can depart this life in equal serenity and peace.

R. N. Creasy

The Suburban Housewife

THE Women's Section of the BUF, which I joined in 1933, was large, enthusiastic and very active. It had its own drum corps, one member of which was the wife of the Movement's Assistant Director-General. The women's drum corps took part in marches all over Britain.

The original Leader of the Women's Section, Lady Esther Makgill, a vivacious redhead, was succeeded in 1933 by Mosley's mother, Maud. Whereas most of us were somewhat overawed by Mosley himself, we were perfectly at ease with his mother, who was easily approachable and motherly. Sometime after our National Headquarters moved from Chelsea to Westminster, Maud, Lady Mosley was in turn succeeded by, I think, a Miss Shore. The Women's Leader I recall most vividly is Anne Brock-Griggs, the tall, blonde and elegant wife of an architect. She contested Limehouse in the London County Council elections of 1937, receiving some 2,000 votes, and remained Leader of the Women's Section for the remainder of the BUF's existence.

'Real sex equality' was one of the BUF's tenets. This has not yet been fully secured but was a very long way off in the 1930s. The Representation of the People Act of 1918 had given the Parliamentary vote to women - but only from the age of 30. In that same year women were granted the right to sit in the House of Commons, and appropriately enough - for it was the United States that first gave the vote to women - the American-born Viscountess Nancy Astor became the first woman to take her seat in Parliament - a year after the Election that saw Mosley returned for Harrow. Mosley had assisted Lady Astor's campaign in Plymouth by speaking on her behalf.

Women were effectively barred from executive positions in commerce, industry and government. The fact that there were "3 million surplus women" partly due to a turn-of-the-century excess of female births but mainly caused by the deaths of sweethearts and husbands in the First World War did not make it easy for any of us to get jobs. It was considered rather unnatural for women to take an active interest in politics.

The BUF's support for Women's Rights brought it recruits from women who had somehow made their mark against all the odds. Among these were three famous former suffragettes: Mary Allen, Norah Elam and Mary Richardson.

Mary Allen, daughter of the Manager of the Great Western Railway, was co-founder and subsequent Commandant of the Women's Police Service, later called the Women's Auxiliary Service. She had been won over to the suffragette cause by Annie Kenney, who with Christabel Pankhurst had been roughly thrown out of a meeting in Manchester in 1905 for their impertinence in asking Sir Edward Grey if a Liberal government would give the vote to working women. For her war work, Mary Allen was awarded the Order of the British Empire in 1917. Before policewomen were appointed she codified their duties so that they were ready to handle child welfare and the protection of girls against immoral influences when they began their operations in 1920. She then trained policewomen in Europe.

Mary Richardson, one of the most militant suffragettes, was arrested 9 times in 1913 and 1914 and was one of the first two suffragettes to be forcibly fed. She achieved notoriety by jumping on the running board of King George V's carriage to present a petition and by slashing the 'Rokeby Venus in the National Gallery.

Both Allen and Mary Richardson wrote books describing their experiences. Other well-known women who joined or supported the BUF were Queen Mary's lifelong friend, Viscountess

Dorothy Downe, Lady Clare Annesley, Lady Howard of Effingham, Lady Pearson and Fay Taylour the racing motorist.

Believing as we did in the equality of the sexes, we took part in the same political activities as the men: sales drives, leaflet distribution, whitewashing our slogans on walls, door-to-door canvassing, meetings and marches. And in much the same leisure activities too: cycling, cricket, swimming, athletics, fencing and judo (with Japanese Budokwai instructors), even football and flying. Boxing was one of the few exceptions.

Despite a war-damaged leg which made him limp, Mosley was a first-rate swordsman with sabre, epee and foil and was a member of the British team in the 1937 world championship contest held in Paris. He was a formidable fencer with words too, as some lawyers found to their cost. Several of his courtroom ripostes have passed into legal lore and history.

Cross-examined at Lewes Assizes in October 1934 by a frustrated and needled prosecuting counsel who angrily demanded: "Will you answer yes or no?" Mosley replied "I will give evidence in my own way, and I do not require any instruction from you." "Don't be offensive" protested Counsel. "To be offensive is not the prerogative of a King's Counsel" was Mosley's reply.

In Mosley's case against *The Star*, the defending Counsel, Norman Birkett, asked: "Supposing a communist government was in power with the consent of the King, would you still oppose it with guns?" Mosley replied: "You might as well ask me what would happen if the King enacted the law of Herod and ordered every first-born in the land to be killed. The question is so hypothetical as to be absurd."

Apart from the BUF's policy of "real sex equality" many women were attracted to it by Mosley's determination to keep Britain out of all foreign wars. As early as 1919 he had opposed the sending of an expeditionary force against the Bolsheviks, and after the Spanish Civil War broke out he ordered his followers not to fight for Franco. The BUF's peace campaigns from 1935 on, with their slogans: Mind Britain's Business, Britons Fight for Britain Only, and The War on Want is the War We Want, had a strong appeal to women who had endured the suffering and horror of the First World War, and had in many instances been widowed by it.

There were, I think, two main reasons why the majority of men and women joined the BUF and they were the same reasons for which millions supported similar movements throughout Europe: (1) the belief that for the first time in history the social evils of poverty and unemployment could be remedied by determined men using the powers of modern science; and (2) the conviction that Soviet Communism was the greatest threat that the West had ever faced, and that only a counter-dynamism could possibly hold it in check.

After 1935, when the danger of a Communist revolution in Britain had receded, our Movement was reorganised on a constituency basis to fight municipal and parliamentary elections, and many of us attended lectures on electoral law and proceedings. These lectures were given both at National Headquarters and at branch offices. A course for election agents was even given by post. Almost a hundred prospective Parliamentary candidates were chosen, including quite a number of women, among them Lady Pearson for Canterbury and Joan Reeve for an East Anglican constituency.

In 1936 the BUF held a Summer Camp at Selsey in Sussex. This was attended by 1,200 Blackshirts from all over Britain. On the last Sunday of the camp there was quite a motorcade of coaches, cars, motor-cycles and bicycles on the main road leading from London containing members on their way to the camp for a day trip. It was gloriously sunny. Standing outside a tent in the youth section of the camp was Mosley's son, Nicholas, bespectacled, aloof and already wearing an expression of disapproval. A young

Blackshirt, Donald Chambers, had been assigned the duty of keeping an eye on him and making sure he was not pestered.

In 1938 when the Czech crisis arose, Mosley declared: "I don't care if 3½ million Germans from Czechoslovakia go back to Germany. I don't care if 10 million Germans go back to Germany. Britain will still be strong enough, brave enough, to hold her own."

In April, 1939, with the war clouds gathering rapidly, our paper *Action* predicted that England could not emerge victorious from another European war; that America and Russia would have to be drawn in and that victory would go to international finance and Bolshevism.

Between the outbreak of war in September 1939 and May 1940, our campaign to secure an honourable peace while this was still possible was conducted mostly by the women members and the older men, our young men having been called up. Urged by Labour politicians such as Attlee, Greenwood and Morrison, a Government that had never understood what the BUF was all about put Mosley behind bars. Mosley's doubting son, Nicholas has put it rather well:

"Labour politicians - perhaps because their feelings of loyalty are apt to be divided between party, nation, internationalism and class - sometimes seem vengefully to need the scalps of those who they feel have betrayed them. They had not forgiven Mosley for having been what they called a 'traitor' to their party in 1930; they now had a chance to suggest he might be a traitor to his country."

So the senseless war continued, and the number of women "doomed by this war conspiracy to the bitterest tears that a woman can shed" to quote Mosley, grew to tens of millions all over the world.

Careful examination of events before Mosley's arrest is revealing indeed. Neville Chamberlain resigned as Prime Minister on 10th May and was immediately appointed Lord President of the Council with a seat in an inner War Cabinet by his successor, Winston Churchill. It had been a busy day. Clement Attlee, Leader of the Labour Party and Arthur Greenwood, Deputy Leader, had returned from the Party Conference at Bournemouth - where Mosley's detention had been one of the main topics - and had discussions first with Chamberlain and then with Churchill. That same evening Churchill, Chamberlain, Halifax, Attlee and Greenwood became the five members of the War Cabinet. A day or two later, Herbert Morrison was appointed Minister of Supply.

Sir John Anderson, Home Secretary and Minister of Home Security, did not regard the BUF as a danger to national security and he opposed the mass internment of British subjects. On 18th May he reported to the Cabinet:

"Although the policy of the British Union of Fascists is to oppose the war and to condemn the Government, there is no evidence that they would be likely to assist the enemy. Their public propaganda strikes a patriotic note ... In my view it would be a mistake to strike at this organisation at this stage by interning the leaders."

Churchill, however, was receiving very different advice from other quarters, especially from certain individuals and groups whose motives ranged from the slightly suspicious to the utterly discreditable.

Chamberlain is not likely to have forgotten the humiliation inflicted on him by Mosley in 1924, when he only just scraped in against Mosley at Ladywood with a 72 majority, after 2 recounts.

Attlee and Greenwood had not forgiven Mosley for leaving the Labour Party in 1930. They wanted the German refugees to be released from detention and Mosley and the leading members of the BUF interned in their place.

The Cabinet had also received an alarming report from the Joint Intelligence Committee. This Committee had failed to anticipate the German attack on Norway, which pre-empted a British occupation of that country. The JIC described in detail how Hitler's 'Fifth Column' in Norway had committed numerous acts of sabotage to aid the Germans. (After the war, the distinguished Dutch historian, Louis de Jong was given the task of writing an official UNESCO report on the activities of these Norwegian traitors. He began his task with enthusiasm, expecting that what he uncovered would be sensational. And so it was, but not in the way he expected: he found that a Norwegian Fifth Column had never existed).

The Joint Intelligence Committee was quite sure that Hitler had his Fifth Column in Britain. Where could it be? It might be hiding among the 73,000 German refugees or within the 20,000-strong Communist Party or among the 9,000 known members of the BUF or the large Irish community. Or perhaps it was split up among all these. The fact that not a single act of sabotage had occurred in Britain might have led an ordinary mortal to deduce that Hitler's Fifth Column in Britain did not exist. The professional plotters who composed the JIC knew better.

On 22nd May Chamberlain (Churchill being in France) announced to Halifax, Attlee and Greenwood that traitors had been found and were in collusion with a Tory MP. These 'traitors' were a cipher clerk at the American Embassy, an isolationist who had discovered that Roosevelt was engaging in activities for which he could be impeached by the House of Representatives, and the daughter of a Tsarist Russian admiral. The MP had intended to ask questions in the House of Commons that would have revealed Roosevelt's duplicity to the world. The Cabinet were unanimous. They had found an excuse to silence Mosley. The law was changed overnight. From the morning of 23rd May,

1940, every one of the 9,000 known members of the BUF could be imprisoned indefinitely without charge or trial - because Mosley had met Hitler in 1936.

As Mosley himself pointed out later, at the time of his arrest 4 out of 5 of the BUF's branch organisers were already serving in the Armed Forces, as were the majority of the young male members. With a few rather shocking exceptions - such as the airman who had been wounded while taking part in the RAF's raid on the Kiel Canal on 4th September, 1939 - hardly any of the Servicemen were detained. The majority of those who were imprisoned were the older members, many of them ex-Servicemen who had been wounded and disabled (several had lost arms and legs) in the First World War, and the very young: lads of 18 and 19 who had not yet been called up.

Considering the size of the Women's Section, the number of women detained was also quite small. At the top were Lady Diana Mosley (who had never taken part in her husband's political activities), Anne Brock-Griggs, Leader of the Women's Section, Mrs. N. Dacre-Fox, a Headquarters administrator, and the wives of various leading members, such as Mrs. De Laessoe. Young women speakers on whose shoulders our Peace Campaign had largely fallen because the men speakers were mostly in uniform, were a particular target, despite the Home Secretary's assurance to Parliament that national security was the reason for the clamp-down and not our propaganda activities for peace.

Our Edinburgh branch had some exceptionally fine members. The women's organiser had joined the Women's Royal Naval Service (the WRENS) as an officer immediately on its formation at the outbreak of war. Neither she nor any other of our women members in the Armed Services was imprisoned. Then as now, military commanders tended to regard politicians' directives as cynically inspired, and to be treated with considerable doubt.

Ann Page

The Dorset Farmer

ONE-FIFTH of the world, one-quarter of its population, were within an Empire built by men from a group of small islands off the coast of Europe. What an achievement! How proud one was to be British! How difficult it is for those of us old enough to recall those days and to recapture that feeling. How impossible it must be for those born since to even begin to understand.

Proud to be British we were in the 1930s . . . and yet . . . and yet. Within that vast Empire every conceivable raw material could be found; every element for wealth production existed. Yet all was not well. Britain had a large proportion of her people unemployed and suffering a depth of poverty quite unknown today. Her position as a world power was being undermined by largely unilateral disarmament which left her with inadequate military defences. Her agriculture was being depressed by imports of cheap food which ruined her farmers and left them to face bankruptcy without hope.

It was this burning patriotism, coupled with an equally burning indignation with an unacceptable economic system and with inept politicians who had no answers to the nation's pressing problems, that caused many, including myself, to rally to Mosley.

In 1930 I was twenty and had read and puzzled quite a lot about the problems which faced Britain and the world. In the 1931 General Election I voted Liberal for the only time in my life. I did so because East Dorset was one of only two constituencies in the country where a National Liberal opposed a Tory. Although I had been brought up a Tory and all my family voted Tory, I had come to believe that Britain needed a National Government, above party politics. The so-called "National Government" which came into existence under Ramsay MacDonald proved to be merely a front for the Tories and the nation's problems remained unsolved.

In the autumn of 1933, on visiting close family friends, I found to my astonishment that the oldest son (who was my own age) had a copy of *The Blackshirt* and was loud in praise of Sir Oswald Mosley. I was astonished because he was a great joker and until then I thought there was not a single serious side to his character, but on this particular subject he was perfectly serious.

He gave me his copy of *The Blackshirt* and after reading it I wrote off for Mosley's book *The Greater Britain.* A touch of 'flu gave me the opportunity to read it carefully from cover to cover and I found it advocated so many of the things my mind had been moving towards over the previous two or three years. What were these things?

Firstly, an economic policy of increased spending power via high wages, made possible by insulating ourselves from the undercutting effect of cheap imported goods and food produced by low-paid labour; a Britain as self-sufficient as possible and an Empire entirely so. To me, a farmer, an expanded home agriculture to produce food which at that time was so largely imported made an especial appeal. Secondly, a sturdy belief in Britain and her Empire, and in the future of both. Britain would retain her Empire, but would give the indigenous peoples an increasing voice in the running of their own affairs. Thirdly, a real attempt to preserve peace in a way more realistic than the fuddled operations of the League of Nations. Peace would be preserved by Britain minding her own business and never fighting another war except in her own defence, and by reaching an understanding with the other European nations.

The Greater Britain said much, much more, but these were the particular policies which made the greatest impact on my mind as being sensible and overdue. I joined the British Union of Fascists.

Although I soon developed a thick hide, I was at that time a shy and sensitive individual who had been brought up to be "respectable". It therefore took quite an effect of will to make oneself conspicuous by donning a black shirt and to risk drawing ridicule or shame on self and family by selling political newspapers in the street - of all things !

Before long I went off for a week's training at the "Black House" in King's Road, Chelsea. One night I volunteered to act as a steward at an outdoor meeting in the East End. Our speaker was an able youngster, still in his 'teens. His audience was quite unlike anything I had ever seen or experienced. It consisted largely of a raving, ranting mob, which threatened to charge the platform and beat up the speaker. We stewards surrounded the platform to keep the hostile crowd at bay. The speaker, able as he was, had no chance of making himself heard. After a while a spokesman for the hostile part of the crowd said that if he was permitted to use our platform for ten minutes he would promise that thereafter our speaker would be given a fair hearing. Unwisely our speaker agreed. It soon became clear that the hostile section of the crowd were Communists and that it was their leader who had taken over the platform. Ten minutes passed but there was no stopping him. When at last he did give way and our speaker resumed, the shouting and threats were every bit as violent as before. This incident made an impact on me that I have never forgotten. In my search for an answer to Britain's problems before I joined the BUF I had made a study of Communism.

True I had rejected it, but I could see some of the arguments in its favour. But I had been brought up to believe that an Englishman's word was his bond and took pride in the fact; this experience taught me that whatever theoretical merit Communism might have, to the Communist ends justified means, and that consequently Communists can in no way be trusted. All my experiences since then have confirmed that early view.

The first large meeting which I attended was at the Albert Hall and the second at Olympia. We marched to Olympia from Chelsea and found another howling mob who had been brought from all parts of the country with the well-publicised intention of preventing us from holding the meeting. Inside the hall there was early chaos, because the Reds had forged tickets and the stewards had trouble sorting out who had valid tickets and whose tickets were forged.

I was allocated duty on a door leading to a small enclosed yard at the rear of the hall, which had large doors leading onto the street. It was a quiet spot and I could watch what was happening in the hall itself. Almost as soon as the meeting started groups of interrupters commenced shouting, first from one spot and then from another. This was not ordinary heckling but continuous, persistent shouting, designed to prevent the audience around them from hearing the speaker and to distract everyone's attention from what was being said. After several warnings, the stewards moved to eject them. The interrupters resisted and fights ensued. Gradually one group after another was removed. My part in all this was to open the street doors so that the Reds could be thrown out. As the struggle went on and tempers rose, "thrown" was the operative word. But the responsibility for such treatment was clearly with those who came to try to prevent a perfectly lawful meeting from being held and resisted violently when asked to leave. They failed. In the end all interrupters were removed. A large and attentive audience then listened to a remarkable speech by a remarkable man. They responded to it with enthusiasm.

The next day, newspapers and radio contrived to give the impression that we were somehow responsible for interrupting our own meeting and even for the mob which tried hard to prevent any of the audience reaching the hall! This was such a distortion of the facts that I began to realise how dirty a game politics is when played by those who control the media.

I went on to become an organiser and speaker myself, taking meetings indoors and out, rough and smooth. I even studied the law to qualify as an election agent.

In this way I came to know many of the leading people in our organisation. These included William Joyce. He was efficient and courageous but an egoist. Although "Director of Propaganda" he converted few people. As a speaker he had his own style: a considerable command of language, but always biting and sarcastic. He amused members with his scathing attacks on all who did not agree with us, but his personality and manner repulsed many who were attracted by our policies and ideas when presented by those with a more pleasant and persuasive approach. Mosley was quite right to expel him as he was doing the Movement great harm.

Joyce was really only concerned with his insatiable need to appear in the limelight. It was this egoism which caused him to become a traitor and to broadcast for Germany during the war. I well remember my feeling of embarrassment and disgust when I recognised his unmistakable voice over the German radio two or three days before our press identified him. That anyone who had ever been associated with us and professed to share our intense patriotism could aid our country's enemies in this way, no matter how much they thought the war mistaken, seemed quite incredible. But at the time I underestimated Joyce's egotism, which for several years after his expulsion from the BUF (for disloyalty) had had no platform in Britain from which to project itself. In the end, he went bravely to his death, condemned as Professor A. J. P. Taylor put it, for making a false declaration on a passport application.

Then there was Alexander Raven Thomson, a man of a very different character. A brilliant writer and speaker, he was essentially an intellectual, who was nevertheless prepared to become fully involved in the rough and tumble of a practical political movement. I came to have an enormous liking and respect for him. He helped me to become a speaker, both at formal speakers' schools and in a quite unintentional way. He was due to address an indoor meeting in a local market town. Quite a large audience had assembled to hear him. The meeting was due to start but there was no sign of him. Instead a telegram arrived to say that he had been directed to the wrong train and would be arriving late. My colleagues insisted that I should have to open the meeting and keep talking until he arrived, as I had been to one short session at a speakers' school and no-one else had even this pretension as a speaker. I had never before addressed an indoor meeting and my mind went blank! However, picking up one of our pamphlets, *Ten Points of Fascist Policy*, I went on to the platform, explained that our speaker would be a few minutes late, and began to expand hesitantly on the policy points one by one. An hour and a quarter later, when I could think of little else to say, Raven Thomson strode into the hall, to my great relief - and no doubt to that of the audience.

I can still picture Raven striding up and down the platform like a caged lion, while words poured from him. It was a brilliant speech and a brilliant performance from a most likeable and clearly very able man. In spite of its inauspicious beginning, the meeting turned out to be a great success. What in retrospect seems remarkable about it is that such was the interest in Mosley's policy that not a single member of the audience left the meeting during what must have been a most tedious hour listening to my faltering efforts while waiting for Raven Thomson to arrive.

A third leading BUF personality who I came to know well was Jorian Jenks, our Movement's agricultural policy adviser. He looked what he had indeed been: a typical yeoman farmer. Forced out of farming by the Depression he had made a name for himself as a writer on rural matters. In 1939 he published Spring Comes Again, in which he outlined his own philosophy and described how this had led him to support Mosley. As a farmer myself I found this a particularly attractive book. Jorian and I had many a friendly argument. He was all for the small farmer and organic farming: I tended to support the more orthodox view. But both of us were firmly united in believing that Mosley's policy of expanding home food production provided the only hope of salvation for British farming. It was also an urgently needed safeguard against starvation should war unfortunately come. After the war we both served on the Rural Reconstruction Association's Research Committee, which studied the practicality of Britain feeding herself. Our conclusions were published in a book entitled *Feeding the Fifty Million*. Jorian later wrote a further interesting book, *From the Ground Up* and became editor of the Soil Association's journal, *Mother Earth*.

At the time of the Abdication crisis, the BUF embarked on a great nationwide campaign, the theme of which was: "Stand By the King". Although individual opinions may have been divided about Edward VIII's wish to marry Mrs. Simpson, we were all in loyal support of the King. He clearly believed in many of the things we believed in: in Britain and her Empire; in the need for real action to relieve the desperate poverty of the poor, especially the unemployed; in avoiding another war, except in self-defence, and consequently in not picking a quarrel with Germany. As a constitutional monarch he could have done little more than bring his personal influence to bear, but this would have been powerful. With his charisma he had an appeal to ordinary people which politicians like Baldwin feared, but which we welcomed. However the combined forces of reaction and hypocrisy proved too powerful, with the sad result that Edward abdicated on 11th December, 1936, after a reign of only 327 days.

With the ever-growing threat of another world war, we embarked on another great campaign, this time for peace. We were passionately of the opinion that Britain should not become involved in the horrors of war unless she was herself attacked. Mosley had advocated such a policy almost ever since he returned from fighting in the First World War - long before Hitler, or even Mussolini, had come to power. Germany had re-armed, Britain had not. We knew that Hitler's quarrel was with Marxism and Soviet Communism and not with Britain. Let Germany seek its Lebensraum in the east. Let Germany and Russia fight it out and in doing so remove the threat of Communism from the rest of the world, while Britain rearmed so as to always be able to resist any attack: such a policy seemed both commonsense and patriotic. To become involved in war, on the other hand, was to risk defeat; but even if we won, Communist Russia - which at that time looked likely to remain neutral - would emerge as a dominant world power, while Britain's position would be greatly weakened.

Our peace campaign reached its climax on 16th July 1939, with the largest indoor meeting ever held anywhere in the world. This was in the huge Exhibition Hall at Earls Court. It was packed to capacity with an enthusiastic audience demanding that peace be maintained. A few weeks later, Chamberlain's government declared war, in support of its fatuous and worthless guarantee to Poland.

The outbreak of the war put us in a most difficult position. As patriots we wished to do nothing which could harm our country or cause it to lose the war, however mistaken we believed that war to be. Yet we were constantly told that the war was being fought to preserve freedom of thought and speech, and that everyone in Britain was free to say what he believed without fear or favour. This being so, we could hardly remain silent, as we profoundly believed that it was in Britain's interest to make an honourable peace while the "phoney" period of the war persisted. So those of us who had not been called to serve in the Forces - mostly the very young, the women and the old - continued to hold meetings at which we urged such a course on our countrymen.

Had the Government felt that such activities were against the interest of the country, they had only to make them illegal and thus suspend free speech for the duration of the war. They did not do so. Instead they arrested Mosley and some hundreds of us his supporters under Regulation 18B. We were not accused of breaking any law or even of intending to do so. Nevertheless we were kept in prisons and concentration camps for many months and even years - something which the politicians said could only happen in countries with the kind of regimes that Britain was fighting to destroy!

Thus the voice of one of the ablest Englishmen of the Twentieth Century was silenced and his outstanding talents wasted. Thus Britain embarked on a disastrous policy, which was to destroy her Empire and undermine her position as a world power; which was to reduce the standard of living of her people to below that of the countries she went to war to defeat; which was to leave capitalist America and Communist Russia in dominant positions over Britain, Europe and the world.

Looking back to our great efforts and struggles in the 1930s to preserve our nation's greatness, we Blackshirts can at least join in saying with sincerity

> 'Tis better to have fought and lost,
> Than never to have fought at all.'

Robert Saunders, O.B.E.

The North London Manufacturer

IN 1934, as a sixteen-year-old apprentice cabinet-maker, I spent many of my lunch hours in Finsbury Pavement, listening to the various political speakers as I munched my sandwiches. It was the Blackshirt speakers who interested me most - men like Patrick Moir and Jock Holliwell - who offered what seemed like a clearly stated and easily understood solution to the enormous problems of unemployment and grinding poverty. If the effort that had gone into war was applied in peace, these problems would soon disappear. Their message was that simple. Despite much heckling these meetings were generally orderly.

My father had been gassed during the First World War, and during the 1920s we lived in two rooms at the top of a three-storey tenement in a poor neighbourhood. But my brother and I were a lot luckier than most of our schoolmates - our father was a yard-foreman with Shell-Mex, earning £3 per week, while our mother had a part-time job as a cook.

In 1936, as an unemployed cabinet-maker, I joined the BUF's Shoreditch branch in Newton Grove. The local organiser was "Duke" Sutherland. My father had always been a strong supporter of the Labour Party, but the bitter political differences that then divided many families did not split ours for the reason that my father combined quite an admiration for Mosley with an intense dislike of 'Bolshies'. Eventually the years of violent coughing caused by wartime gassing took its toll. Father died at the early age of 52, just after Dunkirk.

I was a very active member of the BUF right from joining, attending most regional events and many national ones. During the Spanish Civil War I and other Blackshirts stewarded meetings held by the Friends of National Spain at the Caxton Hall and elsewhere.

I spent a good deal of my time selling our party papers on the street, but there were plenty of other journals that expressed similar viewpoints for us to read.

The Patriot was a political weekly to which some of our members contributed articles and letters. Its readers tended to be people who believed in "conspiracy theories". Truth (motto: "Cultivators of Truth, enemies of Fraud") had an influential readership and could be relied on to expose not only business frauds but Leftwing cant and humbug.

G. K. Chesterton had for many years advocated the widest possible ownership of property through "distributism", publicising such ideas in *G. K.'s Weekly*, which, following his death, was incorporated in *The Weekly Review*.

The New English Weekly, published between April 1932 and September 1949, supported Social Credit but was also quite sympathetic to us. Its editor, A. R. Orage, had made *The New Age* the outstanding literary review before the 1914 War.

The Saturday Review, whose contributors included Max Beerbohm and Bernard Shaw, and which was owned by Lady Houston, published articles by Mosley.

The Criterion, the famous literary review founded and edited by T. S. Eliot and published between 1922 and 1939 was definitely sympathetic to us. Mosley wrote for the *National Review* and the *Quarterly Review*.

Among imported periodicals available to us was the American weekly newspaper *Social Justice*, published by Father Charles Coughlin, the famous Detroit Catholic priest and radio broadcaster who had founded the National Union for Social Justice.

We were influenced in our thinking by the writings of Hilaire Belloc, especially by the prophecies and warnings contained in his books *The Party System* and *The Servile State.* Hilaire Belloc did not join or support our Movement but a number of other famous authors did.

Major Francis Yeats-Brown had served in the cavalry on the North West Frontier of India before the First World War, and was a prisoner of the Turks from 1915 to 1918, an experience he described vividly in his first book. For three years he was Assistant Editor of *The Spectator*, and in 1930 he published his most famous book, *Bengal Lancer*, a partly-autobiographical work. In 1934 he wrote *Dogs of War*, a refutation of pacifism.

Dornford Yates (Major C. W. Mercer) had been called to the Bar in 1909 and in the following year took part in the Old Bailey trial of Dr. Crippen. He served in Egypt in the First World War. Starting with Berry and Co., his slightly farcical novels became very popular and their sales ran into millions. Dornford Yates had no sympathy with the "drab, democratic and mechanized world" of the Twentieth Century, and his novels were designed to bring back a degree of romance into dull lives.

The BUF's most distinguished man of letters was Henry Williamson, who had served as a private in the First World War and who shared Mosley's disillusionment. Williamson made his literary reputation with his 4-volume autobiography, *The Flax of Dreams.* His most famous and successful book, *Tarka the Otter*, won him the Hawthornden Prize. Among his better-known books was *The Story of a Norfolk Farm.* Williamson's political views were expressed openly in his books.

Apart from authors, such entertainers as Harry Champion of "Any Old Iron" fame and the radio humorist, Gillie Potter, belonged to our Movement. We were also strong in musicians, Cuthbert Reaveley being our Director of Music, and G. S. Merriman, the organist at Salisbury Cathedral, composer of one of our songs. These were the kind of people described as "Mosley's thugs"!

One of our best speakers was Jim Shepherd, organiser of Islington branch, to which I transferred in 1939. I remember Mosley addressing a meeting there soon after the declaration of war, asking us to continue our efforts to secure "Peace with Honour". This I did, taking part in demonstrations and paper-selling, but the going became tough - I was slashed with a razor, had pepper thrown in my eyes and suffered several vicious physical assaults.

In January 1940 I joined the Army and became a machine-gunner (Lewis, 1915 vintage) in the Royal Engineers. Four months later we were fighting a desperate rearguard action through France and Belgium. My political comrades seemed a world away, yet unbeknown to me, and quite incredibly, a large number of them were very close indeed.

These were the members of our Bethnal Green, Bow, Limehouse, Shoreditch and Stoke Newington branches who from 1936 on had joined the 1st Battalion of the Rifle Brigade as Regulars and the 1st Battalion of the Queen Victoria Rifles as Territorials in such numbers that one of these became nicknamed in consequence "The Blackshirt Battalion".

After the German armoured divisions had cut the British Expeditionary Force's lines of communication, four battalions of riflemen under the command of Brigadier C. N. Nicholson were despatched to Calais with orders to establish a supply route to Dunkirk. By then the speed of the German advance had made it impossible to establish a route and Brigadier Nicholson received orders to defend the port instead. The Queen Victoria's Rifles was the first battalion to arrive - on 22 May.

On Friday, 24 May, German infantry and the tanks of two Panzer divisions attacked, supported by low-level dive-bombers. By 5 p.m. on the Sunday, the 1st Battalion of the Rifle Brigade was lost to the last man. The QVR's casualties were 116 officers and men.

News of this Thermopylae-like tragedy eventually reached the political prisoners in Peveril Internment Camp on the Isle of Man, where Charles F. Watts, BUF branch organizer for the St. George's Division of Westminster, recorded it in these words:

"One of the four Battalions . . . that held the Germans at Calais long enough to enable the main body of troops to evacuate ... in one of the most heroic rearguard actions of the war was practically 100% Blackshirt - members recruited from East End Districts."

By the vital part they played in delaying the German advance for four days our young Blackshirt dead helped to make possible the ensuing "Miracle of Dunkirk". In so bravely sacrificing their lives for their country they had also given the most convincing answer to those who at that very moment were dubbing us "traitors" and "Fifth Columnists".

After my evacuation from Dunkirk and return to England, I discovered that many of my friends had been imprisoned. I kept in touch with them as best I could, spending the rest of my Army life as a trade instructor at Chatham, until I was invalided out towards the end of 1944 for being C3 - the result of getting in the way of an unfriendly missile in Belgium in 1940.

Though some Brixton Prison warders were reputed to have sheltered beneath Mosley's cell whenever there was an air raid in the naive belief that the Luftwaffe would be careful to avoid dropping bombs on him, the Germans showed no such scruples about bombing the precise areas of East London in which we enjoyed widespread support, and where for years

Mosley's meetings had attracted enthusiastic audiences of tens of thousands.

Whole families of BUF members and supporters were wiped out in Limehouse, Bethnal Green, Bow and Hackney in the heavy raids of 7-8 September 1940, when 600 day and night bombers and fighters attacked the East End over a 12-hour period, and in the assaults that continued without remit for 57 nights.

In Bethnal Green alone, where we had more than a thousand members, some 80 tons of bombs were dropped, and there was enormous damage and loss of life in Hackney, where our two branches, Hackney Central and Hackney South, each had many hundreds of members. During the month of September, 5,730 people were killed and almost 10,000 injured. Further great raids continued until 10 May 1941.

By the war's end, a grievously large number of our members - civilians as well as servicemen - were dead. Whatever the future political climate might be, the voices of many of the BUF's bravest and best - and Britain's bravest and best - had been silenced forever.

Patrick O'Donegan

The Lancashire Baker

IT WAS May 1930, and I was unemployed and living in Southampton. I had moved there from Southport in the hope of finding work as a ship's baker. I was living in lodgings. My dole had just been cut from 17 shillings a week to 15s3d and I often knew what it was to be hungry. My landlady loaned me a copy of The Sunday Express (I could not afford to buy one). The editor had headlined a speech made by a government minister putting forward proposals for dealing with unemployment and attacking the government for failing to tackle the problem. He was one of three ministers who had been directed to find both short and long term plans for unemployment. He was the only one of the three to produce a programme, but it was turned down on the advice of Philip Snowden, Chancellor of the Exchequer, as not being acceptable to the City of London. The name of this minister was Oswald Mosley.

Reading that speech in a borrowed newspaper changed my whole life. Today, after more than 50 years, I count it a privilege to have been numbered among his friends. In recent years I have met many politicians, including the Prime Minister, the Chancellor of the Exchequer, the former Minister of Defence, Michael Heseltine - with whom I once shared a platform in Preston when I had to follow him at the microphone - and Enoch Powell, who I last chatted with on the lawn of Buckingham Palace at a Royal Garden Party. None of these present-day politicians has the natural charisma and personal magnetism of Mosley. When he entered a room, all heads turned.

Mosley's influence was not the only one which finally launched me into political life. Others conditioned my early thinking but he was the catalyst. Politics and economics were a general topic of conversation in my early home life. My Socialist father had walked and talked with Philip Snowden when he was Member of Parliament for Blackburn; with J. R. Clynes who, from being a child worker in a cotton factory, rose to Cabinet rank; and with Jimmy Thomas, a very good union organizer, even though he proved hopeless in high office.

My political grounding was already deeply implanted, but my love of singing was also a contributory factor. Shortly after I moved to Southampton in search of work, the choirmaster of the church I attended asked me to join the choir. It is only quite recently that bronchitis and emphysema have compelled me to abandon this, one of the great joys of my life.

Two contrasting incidents occurred in 1930 which influenced the future pattern of my life. The choirmaster arranged for us to visit Quarr Abbey on the Isle of Wight for a weekend, to receive instruction from the Benedictine monks on the rendering of Gregorian Chant. This music, used in the Latin Sung Mass, is regrettably no longer heard in our churches since the abandonment of the Tridentine Rite. Gregorian Chant is the oldest recorded form of written music in the Christian Church. It possesses a haunting lilt which penetrates the soul. I am still word-perfect in my memory not only of the music but also of the Latin words, my favourite section being the Credo which commences: Credo in Unum Deum, Patrem Omnipotentum, and is the longest section in the entire mass. Very occasionally we are treated to a television broadcast in one of the Sunday services from one of our monasteries and the first bar of the Credo brings it all flooding back. Once again I am in Quarr Abbey singing in unison with the monks which to me is still the most beautiful music in the world.

Eventually I was lucky enough to get a part-time job in a one-shop bakery. In addition to working in the bakery I served in the shop on one day a week. On one of these occasions a poorly-dressed pinch-faced boy came into the shop and asked for a loaf of bread, the price of which was 3½ pence. I gave him the loaf, in return for which he handed me two empty milk bottles (on each of which there was a redeemable deposit of one penny), a one-penny stamp, and a farthing. I didn't ask him for the other farthing. I knew only too well what it was to be hungry and obviously he had given me the only money he had. This small but significant incident illustrates the harsh realities of the Hungry Thirties.

While in Southampton, as a member of the choir of St. Boniface I was invited to join the Knights of St. Columba and also the S.V.P. Society. Membership of the former required study of Pope Leo XIII's Rerum Novarum (The Workers' Charter), an economic treatise laying down the basic Christian requirements for a just society; while membership of the latter, a charitable society, necessitated visiting the sick and aged.

Periodic visits to the workhouse and what I saw in that ghastly establishment prepared the basis of all my future political activity. Mosley's resignation speech brought the culmination of my personal political development. I have no wish to convey the impression that I am a deeply religious person. I am not. If there is a theologian whose intellect and personality I admire it must be Thomas Aquinas, but in all honesty I must confess that I find I have more in common with Thomas (Didymus), "help thou my unbelief".

Life is full of paradoxes. My love of singing helped to keep me in my religious faith. My love of talking and the public platform provided a natural outlet for my political faith. But while the former has waxed and waned, the latter has grown from strength to strength.

In 1931 I returned to Southport, to a good job and a circle of close companions. Our objective was to enjoy life, which we did to the full. Politics were temporarily forgotten, but not for long.

On a Saturday evening in September 1933 I was on my way to the local dance hall where I was to meet my friends. Suddenly from nowhere there appeared a heavily-built man wearing a black shirt. He pushed a newspaper under my nose and said in a strong 'Geordie' accent: "Buy *The Blackshirt*, one penny". Immediately Mosley and his resignation speech of three years before flashed through my mind. I handed over my penny, put the paper in my pocket and continued on to my dance.

On Sunday I remembered it, and read it with growing interest. Rubber-stamped on the front page was the address of the BUF's Southport branch, 51 Houghton Street. I called there the following day, spent most of that evening talking to the local organizer, Harry Jones, and ended by signing a form applying for membership. In the following weeks I met my Blackshirt with the Geordie accent on numerous occasions. It was Tommy Moran, one-time boxing champion of the Royal Navy. At that time he was domiciled in Manchester, as a staff speaker, and a very forceful speaker he was. We became very close friends.

Not long after joining the BUF I was persuaded by Tommy Moran to try public speaking. To my surprise I found that I was a natural. Southport was rather unusual: it had no recognised speaking sites and the local police would not sanction the holding of street corner meetings. In consequence I had to go to the market town of Ormskirk to develop my oratorical talents. Evidently I have not been forgotten in Ormskirk, for when I was helping out in a friend's shop there a few years ago a customer asked me if I had addressed meetings in 1934.

I first met Mosley early in 1934. He specially asked to see me because I had been involved in a street fight with the Reds in Cheetham Hill, Manchester. I had been thrown through the window of a butcher's shop, where I lay with a flowering geranium plant on either side of me. Fortunately I was not seriously hurt.

On two occasions I had the honour of acting as opening speaker for Mosley, once during an indoor meeting in the L.C.C. elections of 1937, and once in Trafalgar Square.

In January 1935 I moved to Hull. During the five years that I lived there I averaged forty meetings a year, often cycling nine miles to Beverley or sixteen miles to Driffield. My usual site in Hull was on the corner of Baker Street and Prospect Street, but I held meetings on all the recognised speaking sites in the city. It was at Baker Street that I was arrested under the Public Order Act for wearing a political uniform, i.e. our "Circle and Flash" armband. Found guilty by the Stipendiary Magistrate I was fined Ten Pounds - a month's wages in those days.

My three brothers and I were all living in different towns and we seldom corresponded. When I went to hear Mosley speak at Leeds Town Hall I found my brothers there, each of us wearing the black shirt. Not one of us knew that the others had joined. We all remained active up to the outbreak of the war. One brother was in a reserved occupation, one joined the merchant navy, one joined the Royal Air Force. I entered Walton Gaol and was not released from political imprisonment until November 1943. As I write this in the summer of 1984, we are all still alive, three of us living in Southport and one in New Zealand.

Soon after moving to Hull I was appointed branch organizer and propaganda officer for East Yorkshire. As two of my brothers were then also living in Hull we jointly rented a very large house, using part of it as our Headquarters. We provided accommodation for many visiting senior officials, including Bill Risdon, Assistant Chief Election Agent, National Inspectors John Sant and John Hone, Raven Thomson, Jorian Jenks, and our own National Inspector for Yorkshire, Peter Whittam. Many others became my friends including Charlie Hammond, Charlie Watts, Mick Clarke and Bob Row, who became editor of the post-war *Action*.

I met Hector McKechnie, national meetings organiser, on a number of occasions, in connection with arrangements for Mosley's meetings in my area. I first met William Joyce on the same day that I met my brothers in Leeds, when he held an impromptu meeting on the steps of Leeds Town Hall. I had heard him speak previously at a meeting at The Stadium, Liverpool, when I had been greatly impressed by his sharp tongue and quick repartee. These qualities were said to repel, but when Joyce debated with Fenner Brockway, political secretary and editor for the Independent Labour Party, at St. Andrew's University, the students voted in favour of the Corporate State and against Socialism, inflicting on Brockway what he later described as the greatest humiliation of his life.

I also met John Beckett, famous for stealing the Mace in the House of Commons while a Labour M.P. He left our Movement with Joyce. Beckett was a clever and impressive speaker. He once deputised for Mosley - who was ill at the time - at a meeting in the Fulford Rooms in Hull. It was at this meeting that I first met the unforgettable Dick Bellamy. In its early stages this meeting had been somewhat noisy, and I was waiting at the back of the hall in anticipation of a break-in by the hundreds of Reds who were clamouring outside. An elderly lady, distressed by the disturbance, wished to leave, and Dick was escorting her to the exit. As soon as I opened the door we were met with a hail of stones. Fortunately the police were in evidence, and they took care of the lady, but Dick and I became involved in a fracas before we were able to re-enter the hall.

Dick Bellamy and I have been the closest of friends since that time and remain so today. We have visited each other over the years and still correspond. He has a charming wife. I once had the privilege of meeting Mosley's mother on the occasion of one of the London marches, when she, with Anne Brock-Griggs, was leading the Women's Section.

I vividly recall my first encounter with our Director General.

Neil Francis Hawkins. It was at Olympia. A member of the Red Front had climbed one of the main girders and was causing a disturbance. Foolishly I started to climb up after him, but Francis Hawkins, who was just behind me, pulled me down. After telling me not to be a fool, he climbed up the girder. When Mosley was speaking at Holbeck Moor, Leeds, Francis Hawkins and I stood on the loudspeaker van holding up the leads to the microphone which the Communists were trying to tear down. Town Moor, Newcastle, was rough but the roughest and toughest meeting that I ever attended was on the Corporation Field, Hull, in 1936. After this meeting, which I had organised, the police collected bicycle chains, brush staves with 6-inch nails in the end, chair legs wrapped with barbed wire and thick woollen stockings containing broken glass in the heels. We had 27 hospital cases and the Communists had over a hundred. It was at this meeting that a bullet was put through the windscreen of Mosley's car. There was so much noise that no-one heard the shot. The following day I carried my speaker's stand down to the labour exchange and held a meeting on my own. Because this was so unexpected I got away with it and was not attacked.

I attended all the major indoor meetings: at the Free Trade Hall in Manchester, the Usher Hall in Edinburgh, all the Albert Hall meetings and finally Earls Court. This was the most spectacular of all and left a lasting impression on my mind. I just did not believe that war was possible after such a mighty demonstration for peace. It is now over fifty years since I committed myself to Mosley and my belief in him still grows with the years. I miss him more than I can say.

John W. Charnley

The South London Reporter

TWO EVENTS, significant to me, occurred in 1919: in London the 22-year old Oswald Mosley made his maiden speech in the House of Commons and in a small village in Lancashire a son was born to one of two blacksmith brothers.

Fourteen years later, I started my first job in a Manchester office. Inspired by a newspaper account of Mosley's address to an 8,000-strong audience at Belle Vue, with his stirring call "Wake Up, you men of England! ", I applied to the BUF's Northern Headquarters for membership, claiming that I was 16. In response I received a visit from 'an old gentleman' - the 35-year-old Victor Marsden, who enrolled me, giving me a membership card and the very first issue of *The Fascist Week*, launched on Armistice Day, 1933.

For the next 3 years I had no personal contact with other members. I propagated our cause by distributing pamphlets around our village and leaving copies of *The Blackshirt* lying around the factory where I then worked.

A record of Mosley's speech at the BUF's first Albert Hall meeting was issued in 1934. I played this to any relative or friend who could be persuaded to listen. I heard it so many times that eventually I knew it by heart, from:

"This great audience is gathered here tonight, filling the largest hall in Britain to hear the creed of the postwar world", to its magnificent ending: "Again and again in the long story of the human race, races have struggled up to nations and nations up to mighty empires; have scaled the heights of history and have thought they were safe; and now lit by the flame of such high inspiration this movement rises from the very soul of England to give all, to dare all, that England may live in greatness and in glory."

When I was nearly 17, I became ill with rheumatic fever and spent several months in hospital. On discharge, at doctor's advice I moved to London with my mother, to escape the damp Lancashire climate. I transferred to our Clapham branch, and attended a meeting of active members in the branch organizer's house in Ferndale Road, called to discuss arrangements for the Movement's Fourth Anniversary Demonstration. It was October 1936. Although I should have worn the grey shirt of our Youth Movement I was given special permission to march with the others, wearing the black shirt.

On Sunday, 4 October 1936, the BUF planned a series of demonstrations in East London, where it had a mass following. Starting at the Royal Mint, several thousand Blackshirts would march through Limehouse, Shoreditch, Bow and Bethnal Green, in each of which Mosley would deliver a speech. Communists and other members of the Hard Left had been preparing for weeks to prevent this march taking place and they erected barricades across Cable Street and other surrounding streets. Sir Philip Game, the Police Commissioner, who was present with 6,000 policemen, ordered them to clear the barricades. After a fierce battle between police and Reds in which stones, bricks and iron bars were used against the police, Cable Street was eventually cleared. To prevent further serious disorder, Sir Philip Game, after securing the Home Secretary's concurrence, ordered the march to be called off. Mosley, law-abiding to a fault, instructed his supporters to turn about, and they marched to the Embankment where they were dismissed.

With other members of Clapham branch, all of us in uniform, I emerged from Mark Lane Underground Station (now called Tower Hill). On the Tube train there had been plenty of verbal altercation with members of the opposition, who were on their way to block our march, but no physical violence. However, outside the station we met Tommy Moran, a former boxing champion of the Royal Navy, one of the few Blackshirts to be injured on that day, his head covered in bandages. He had been hit on the head with a chair leg covered in barbed wire, but being a man whose toughness was legendary, he was not disconcerted in the slightest. He smiled broadly and even happily at us. With him was "Fatty" Fields, another well-known member, a coalman from Bethnal Green.

After our dismissal on the Embankment many of us made our way to the BUF's Headquarters in Great Smith Street, Westminster, where Mosley addressed us from an upstairs window.

"We never surrender," said Mosley. "We shall triumph over the parties of corruption because our faith is greater than their faith, our will is stronger than their will, and within us is the flame that shall light this country and shall later light the world."

The Communist militants, assembled by the coach-load from all over Britain, dispersed, claiming a great victory. Yet a week later we held huge, entirely peaceful meetings throughout East London, culminating on 14 October, when Mosley addressed an audience of 12,000 at Bethnal Green and then marched to Limehouse where he addressed another huge crowd.

My branch held regular weekly meetings at the Polygon and on Clapham Common. My particular job was to deliver our newspapers to non-active members and other subscribers. This I did on my bicycle, carrying several dozen copies in a sling bag on my back, the bag bearing an *Action* slogan. One day someone who apparently did not like the slogan knocked me off my bicycle and gave me a beautiful black eye. I was rather proud of this black eye, and I got our branch organiser, Charles Daniels, to photograph me.

As 1936, and my first four months in London, were drawing to a close, the country was thrown into the Abdication Crisis. I took part in all our "Stand By The King" demonstrations in the West End including the largest one of all, outside Buckingham Palace. In the New Year, a letter from Lt.-Col. C. S. Sharpe, the BUF's Assistant Director-General, informed me that I had been accepted for membership of the elite N. I. Division.

We celebrated May Day 1937 with the biggest march we had ever held in East London, from Bethnal Green to Limehouse, where Mosley spoke, and promised to revive the happy and wholesome life of Merrie England.

In 1937, as recognition for my devoted service, I received a special certificate signed by the BUF's Director-General, Neil Francis-Hawkins, and known as "Steel Distinction".

In the Spring of that same year the Labour Party held a rally in Hyde Park in support of the Spanish Republicans. The BUF decided to hold a mass sales drive in nearby Park Lane, and there was an inevitable clash in which one Blackshirt, "Dixie" Dean, was thrown into a basement.

In 1938 I transferred to our Battersea branch, whose organizer was Albert Wyles and whose headquarters were in Lavender Hill. Our principal branch speaker was Albert Muirhead, and our prospective Parliamentary candidate was Captain Charles Bentinck-Budd, one of the BUF's National Inspectors. George Dunlop from Limehouse branch was a frequent guest speaker. It was in Battersea branch that I met my future wife. She had been a member of the New Party before joining the BUF.

In October 1938 I went north for a long weekend, to hear Mosley speak at the Free Trade Hall in Manchester on a Saturday evening, and to visit my native village. Returning to work on Tuesday, having taken Monday 'off', I was instantly dismissed. This was how I came to meet our Industrial Adviser, P. G. Taylor, who was successful in obtaining for me a week's salary in lieu of notice.

P. G. Taylor did a good job at NHQ and was well liked. But he was not all that he appeared to be. Indeed he was not "P. G. Taylor" at all but a member of MI5. Mosley knew this, because "P. G. Taylor" openly admitted it to him, but Mosley, who had absolutely nothing to hide, could see the humour of the situation. So P. G. Taylor" retained his job.

Membership of the BUF was open to all races and we had Anglo-Indians and Gibraltarians in our ranks. Battersea branch had a Jewish member, Lew Levisohn, who took part in all our activities. Though then unemployed, Lew later won fame and fortune as the husband and manager of the internationally known black 'honkey-tonk' pianist, Winifred Attwell.

I suffered a great disappointment in the summer of 1939. On Sunday, 16 July, the BUF was to hold its greatest-ever indoor meeting, in the huge new Auditorium at Earls Court, and I was looking forward to attending this momentous event, when Mosley would address an audience of up to 30,000 people.

A few days before, an official-looking envelope addressed to me dropped through the letter-box. A few months earlier, a compulsory military service Act had been passed by Parliament, establishing a conscript force called the Militia. I had been conscripted into this body and had to report to Guildford on Saturday, 15 July. I wrote a hasty letter to the Commanding Officer, asking for a week's postponement of my call-up as I had an urgent "private engagement". Not surprisingly, my letter met with a refusal.

In my training platoon I met another BUF supporter, a young man named Irving, whose family were street traders in Hoxton, and we became friends. Neither of us made any secret of our political beliefs. Less than a year later, Irving was killed in the

Battle of France. In the Army I also met George Lambert, a member of our Shoreditch branch. George later won the Military Medal.

Immediately on the outbreak of the Second World War Mosley issued the following "Message to All British Union Members":

"The Government of Britain goes to war with the agreement of all the Parliamentary parties. British Union stands for peace. Neither Britain nor her Empire is threatened. Therefore Britain intervenes in an alien quarrel. In this situation we of British Union will do our utmost to persuade our British people to make peace.

"Before war began, in our struggle for peace, our thousands of members had awakened great masses of the British people to demand peace. But sufficient of the people could not be awakened in time without the money which we did not possess . . .

"To our members my message is plain and clear. Our country is involved in war. Therefore I ask you to do nothing to injure our country, or to help any other power.

"Our members should do what the law requires of them; and, if they are members of any of the Forces or Services of the Crown, they should obey their orders, and, in every particular, obey the rules of the Service. But I ask all members who are free to curry on our work to take every opportunity within your power to awaken the people and to demand peace."

At about this time, Beverley Nicholls, who had written the anti-war classic *Cry Havoc* and who never concealed his admiration for Mosley, made a remarkably prescient entry in his private journal:

"What would the Labour people do now? They had passionately resisted any attempt to enforce conscription. Would they continue to do so? And Oswald Mosley, would they shut him up? And was it not a supreme tragedy that one of the most brilliant men of our age, who might have talked to Hitler in a language that he would have understood, should have been shuffled off the stage as though he were a criminal?"

In October 1939, I heard Mosley speak amid scenes of intense fervour to a huge crowd at Ridley Road, Hackney. I was on army leave and in uniform, as were several other BUF members who I recognized in the audience. A few days later I attended Mosley's packed indoor meeting at the Stoll Theatre in Kingsway. This was my last physical involvement with the BUF.

Some months later, as I lay in the military wing of a London hospital, I received a visitor who, without speaking, threw a copy of The Evening News on my bed. On the front page in banner headlines were the words: "Mosley arrested".

It is a curious fact that neither I nor any other member of my own branch was ever detained, though many members of neighbouring branches such as Brixton were. It is another example of the apparently random and indiscriminate way in which the Emergency Powers were applied. One hopes that the Government will do better if it ever cracks down on real internal enemies.

Some of my comrades who were jailed have since said to me that the Government was right, in a desperate military situation, to act against anyone whose loyalties it regarded as doubtful. But it should have been better informed about the motivation of the BUF's membership, and when, after intense investigation and interrogation, nothing incriminating had been discovered, all those arrested should have been released. But they were useful scapegoats, and many stayed in prison for years, even to the end of the war. The leaders of Labour, wily as well as vindictive, realised that the mere fact of having been imprisoned, in a country where for centuries such treatment was accorded only to the guilty, would damn the interned members of the BUF in the eyes of the general public. And all the time that the finger of suspicion was pointed at us, Communist traitors in the Foreign Office were passing the nation's vital secrets to Soviet Russia - then allied to Germany - by the sackload.

During the Second World War thousands of British Blackshirts served in Britain's Armed Forces, many being killed or wounded. None of them ever engaged in traitorous activities. The facts are plain to see, for anyone who will remove the blinkers from his eyes and mind.

From 1940 on, it was my firm view that Mosley had been detained not because the Government really doubted his loyalty, but because his policy of "Peace, with the British Empire Intact and Our People Safe" was beginning to gain widespread support. It had been the panic measure of a government gripped by hysteria when faced with the grim realities of a crisis of its own making.

This view was confirmed by two conversations that I had after the war. Beverley Baxter, the Tory M.P. for Wood Green, told me that part of the price that had to be paid for Labour's participation in a 'united Government' was the detention of Mosley and the banning of the BUF.

The other conversation was even more damning. On the night following the 1945 election in which Labour was swept to power I was present at Labour's Victory Party at the Savoy Hotel. Aneurin Bevan was holding forth to a group of idolizers, and tongues loosened as the glasses clinked and the night wore on. The question of Mosley was raised.

Aneurin Bevan replied:

"If we hadn't forced Churchill to imprison Mosley - who knows what he might have achieved? He was getting dangerous. People were beginning to listen to him and agree. He might have forced a quick end to the war and become the alternative force to capitalism. Now he's discredited, but I warn all of you - don't rely on it. Mosley is a man who will never be finished. I must remind you of the complete change in attitudes after the last war towards those very unpopular members of our party like Ramsay Macdonald, who had to resign the party leadership in 1914 because he opposed the war and wanted Britain to take any opportunity of securing a negotiated peace."

The years have rolled by. We live in a very different world, with our people facing the greatest danger in all their history. Many of my generation who during and after the First World War were born too late to see their fathers and whose fathers died too soon to see their sons, will soon themselves be no more. After I too pass through that portal from which no mortal man has ever returned, I hope to be reunited with the companions of my youth - with Lieutenant Fane, R.N., Aircraftsman Charlie Watts, Flight-Sergeant Basil Gill, who joined the RAF after his release from detention and was shot down over Berlin; with Squadron Leader "Tigge" Fitch of Clapham branch who survived a 'ditching' in the English Channel only to be burnt to death in his Mosquito - to join these and so many more in singing once again that song whose words were engraved on all our hearts:

Hark! the sound of many voices,
Echoes through the vale of ages.
Britain listens and rejoices,
Gazing on Tradition's pages.
Patriots: your cry is heeded!
Heroes: death was not in vain!
We to your place have succeeded,
Britain shall be great again!

Edmund Warburton

The Essex Farmworker

MY FATHER was a Yorkshire farm worker. When he was a child a third of all British workers were agricultural labourers and many children under the age of ten, right down to mere toddlers, were employed on farms, for education was not yet compulsory.

In the Great Depression that began in the 1870s, many farmers were ruined by cheap imported grain. My father joined the Colonial Police in the 1880s, and as a consequence I was born in Hong Kong in 1910. From 1915 to 1920 father farmed in Kent. In the latter year he bought a farm at Eye in Suffolk, and I worked on this farm as a ploughboy. From father's death until 1948 I ran this farm in partnership with my brother. I then became a farm foreman, for a short period in Holt, Norfolk, then back at Eye, and was in the Manningtree district of Essex for 15 years. Finally I spent six years as a general farm worker at Langenhoe Hall, Colchester. Thus I have done every kind of farm work in every kind of capacity.

I have always been a strong believer in trade unionism, for in every type of industry and business there are unscrupulous employers who will ill-treat their staff if they can get away with it. For practically the whole of my working life, more than 35 years, I was a member of the Agricultural Section of the Transport and General Workers' Union. At about the time my union was established, the average wage of an agricultural labourer was 17s.6d a week, three shillings of which was paid not in cash but in kind. Up until the outbreak of the First World War, farm workers were the poorest section of the community. Yet despite my union's representation on all official agricultural bodies, the average wage when the Second World War broke out was only 35s, a week.

In 1934, as a Committee Member of the Suffolk Tithepayers' Association, I worked with Albert Mobbs and other Suffolk Farmers' Union supporters in the battle against the extortion of tithes and the enforced sale of farmers' goods.

The present generation knows little about tithes and how bitterly they were resented in bygone days. To quote an old law book they were: "The tenth part of the increase yearly arising from the profits of lands, stocks upon land, and the industry of the parishioners, payable for the maintenance of the parish priest, by everyone who had things titheable, if he cannot show a special exemption". In early times, wheat, woollen cloth and butler would have been paid as tithes. The shire reeves stored these products in tithe barns and the monks used them for their own purposes and also for the relief of the poor and sick.

The following story illustrates just how ridiculous and unfair the tithe system had become by the early part of the Twentieth Century. During the First World War my Father, like hundreds of other Kent farmers, grubbed up his top field to grow the much needed corn, without which the country would have faced starvation. There was a special tax on hops at the time. Although the hop crop no longer existed, my Father and all the others were nevertheless compelled to pay the Hop Tithe.

In the Second Great Depression, tithe had become an intolerable burden on the farming community because it had been assessed at an earlier time when cereal prices were much higher. The Ecclesiastical Commissioners distrained on farmers who could not pay their tithes, sending bailiffs in to seize livestock and implements. These were then sold at local auctions, where paltry prices were generally obtained because they were only bought by friends and neighbours of the distrained farmers. To keep going, farmers had to borrow from banks, The Agricultural Mortgage Corporation and The Public Works Loan Board, and the onerous rates of interest they charged resulted in hundreds of farmers going out of business, leaving farms deserted and uncultivated all over Britain.

The farmworkers thus displaced suffered great hardships through the consequent unemployment. For many of them their main source of food was illegal: poached fish or rabbit and "nicked" potatoes and swedes. As one such man said to me at the time: "It's a Rum 'Un when a man can't get enough grub to eat, Bor", ('Bor' being a Suffolk expression meaning "boy", "mate" or "neighbour").

In 1934, those industrial workers who were lucky enough to receive unemployment benefit got 17 shillings a week if single, 26 shillings for a couple and 2 shillings for each child, but an out-of-work farm labourer did not fare so well. If he had no savings or relatives to support him he had to apply for Poor Law help from the local Public Assistance Committee. Part of any relief granted to him had to come from the local rates, and some PACs considered 16 to 20 shillings a week adequate for a man and wife. If he lived in a tied cottage, he could find himself homeless.

Yet even this represented an improvement on earlier times. Until the very beginning of the Twentieth Century an agricultural labourer was, in effect, tied to his own parish, for if he left it he risked losing his right to parish relief if he fell sick and later in old age. Before the First World War an able-bodied person in need of Poor Law relief had only one recourse: the Union Workhouse.

In my Father's childhood, the women and children in a workhouse were placed under the charge of a gangmaster and hired out to various farmers to work on the land. These infamous "Agricultural Gangs" only died out in the 1880s.

When Wortham Manor, a farm on the border of Norfolk and Suffolk, was under threat of distraint I went along to lend support. This was the farm of Mr. Rash, husband of the well-known East Anglian novelist, Doreen Wallace. There I came across a group of Blackshirts, who under the command of Dick Plathen had come down from London to give us a hand. I got into conversation with these men, found their policy for overcoming the agricultural depression sensible, and bought their literature.

Dick Plathen and his colleagues had taken legal advice before coming down to Suffolk and had been told that if they were present at an enforced sale with the farmer's permission and hindered the bailiffs without using force, they would be within the law. So they felled trees across the private road leading to the farm buildings, dug trenches and put up barbed wire. All this attracted nationwide attention and many newspaper reporters and photographers arrived on the scene.

Then police reinforcements were brought in and the Blackshirts were arrested under a long-forgotten statute. They were taken to Mousehold Heath prison, Norwich, and found themselves in the Assize Court, where they were bound over.

I was extremely indignant about these arrests and with others, including my brother, decided to join the local branch of the BUF. A year or two later I became branch treasurer.

The good work of Plathen and his 30 colleagues bore fruit. The adverse press and radio publicity taught the Ecclesiastical Commissioners a lesson. Forcible sales soon ended. In 1936, the greatly disliked rentcharge was abolished, and the Ecclesiastical Commissioners, Queen Anne's Bounty and other tithe-owners were compensated with Government stock.

From 1935 on I attended many BUF meetings in Suffolk and Norfolk and took part in various marches in London. At the BUF's great indoor meeting at Earl's Court in the summer of 1939 I was a standard bearer.

Earl's Court was the largest indoor meeting ever held anywhere in the world. The huge audience was not merely attentive: it was highly enthusiastic. Those who claim that the BUF declined to insignificance after 1934 cannot explain how a dwindling party could have staged such an event. The press and BBC, which for several years had followed a policy of only mentioning our meetings if there had been disturbances at them, ignored this momentous demonstration. The issues at stake were the great issues of war and peace; the speaker was one of Britain's two greatest Twentieth Century orators; yet nothing of what he said was reported in the national newspapers. Britain's "free, democratic press" has a lot to answer for.

Earl's Court proved to be our last great indoor meeting. After speaking for two hours without a break and without notes, Mosley concluded by saying:

"This heritage of England, by our struggle and our sacrifice, again we shall give to our children. And with that sacred gift, we tell them that they come from that stock of men who went out from this small island in frail craft across storm-tossed seas to take in their brave hands the greatest Empire that man has ever seen; in which tomorrow our people shall create the highest civilisation that man has ever known. Remember those who through the centuries have died that Britain might live in greatness, in beauty and in splendour . . .

"To the dead heroes of Britain in sacred union we say - like you we give ourselves to England: across the ages that divide us - across the glories of Britain that unite us - we gaze into your eyes and we give to you this holy vow: We will be true - today, tomorrow and forever - England lives !"

In my old age I find that all the lies told about us in the press and on the radio in the 1930s are repeated in the history books. I hope that the honest testimony given by myself and others in this book will enable fair-minded people to arrive at the truth. We suffered unprecedented abuse - when our sole aim was to keep Britain GREAT.

George Hoggarth

The Birmingham Schoolteacher

IN 1935, at the age of 20, I arrived in Birmingham to take up my first teaching appointment after leaving Training College. My local Education Authority had granted me a loan to get through college, and this loan had to be paid back during my first year's teaching.

As a student of history I had become interested in contemporary politics. I had a leaning towards a vague kind of Utopian Socialism. I was appalled by the economic conditions that I found in Birmingham. I had never seen anything like the back-to-back slum houses existing in parts of the city. Something needed to be done as a matter of urgency, but the Labour Party with its "pie-in-the-sky" attitude seemed more interested in international affairs than in Britain's internal problems. Action was needed now, and action required a political leader of outstanding intelligence, energy and vision. I could see no-one like that in the Labour Party.

Mosley's constructive 'Birmingham Proposals' of 1925 had not been forgotten by the people of Birmingham. I soon heard about them and decided that his policies represented socialism at a national level - a highly patriotic kind of socialism - and that I should join his movement.

This I did in 1936, enrolling at the BUF's local branch in Stafford Street. On the ground floor was a bookshop open to the public, where our literature and journals and books of general political interest were on sale. On the first floor above was the branch organizer's office where he could see members and prospective members, and other rooms used for members' meetings, speakers' schools, etc.

At the time I joined, the Movement was undergoing decentralization and paid officials such as National Inspectors, Assistant National Inspectors, and County Inspectors, were being replaced by unpaid volunteers. Birmingham Branch's bookshop and offices were manned by voluntary workers. There was high unemployment even in comparatively prosperous Birmingham, so someone was usually available during the day as well as in the evenings to keep the branch premises open. Even intelligent, highly-skilled men could not obtain work. My own services were soon taken up at weekends.

What kind of people belonged to Birmingham Branch? A wide cross-section of the community: One member was a son of one of the oldest and largest brewers in Birmingham while another was a well-known independent brewer; a well-to-do coal merchant belonged to our Branch, while we also had solicitors, teachers like myself, doctors, bank clerks, newspapermen (both reporters and technical staff), large and small restaurant owners, many small factory owners (these small metal works abounded at the time in Birmingham), office workers, skilled and unskilled factory workers, railway workers (their pay was abominable in the 1930s), shop keepers and shop assistants and busmen. The wearing of the simple black shirt eliminated all feelings of 'class distinction'. The women members were equally diverse: teachers, secretaries, nurses, waitresses, domestic workers, housewives, etc.

Some time after I joined Birmingham Branch, the Women's Organiser had to give up active membership because of ill-health and I took over from her. The BUF's policy of sex equality meant that in many ways the women were not treated as a separate section, being encouraged and expected to take part in any and every activity. Weekly women's meetings were instituted to discuss women's problems and how best they could help in propagating our cause. The women members were very active indeed in selling *Action* on the streets, and in distributing and selling literature at indoor and open-air meetings. Some developed the ability to speak at meetings. Obviously the women members were invaluable at organizing such fund-raising functions as socials and bazaars.

My husband-to-be became Branch Organizer, and later as more branches were opened in and around Birmingham, District Inspector. We devoted all our spare time to the Movement. It was an exciting and hopeful period in which to live.

The outbreak of war in 1939 was a shattering blow to us. It seemed unthinkable that twenty years after the First World War ended Europe should once again be rent apart.

In June 1940, my future husband was imprisoned under Defence Regulation 18B, firstly in Walton Gaol, Liverpool, then in Stafford Prison and afterwards in the internment camps at York Race Course and Peel on the Isle of Man. At the end of 1941 he was released and almost immediately was called up for military service, spending 4½ years in the Army.

In November 1940 I too was arrested. For me it was Holloway Prison and then the women's internment camp at Ramsay on the Isle of Man. After my release (and nearly two years' loss of salary) I was reinstated to teaching in Birmingham.

This is all part of history now, and for me was an enriching experience. Looking at the state of Europe and the world today, and the vast areas of the world that have fallen under the iron sway of Communism, who can say that the policies and prophecies of Oswald Mosley were wrong?

Though the BUF existed for only eight years, the time and effort given to it by its members was remarkable. The majority of active members devoted two nights a week, and a considerable number gave five. Up to 1,000 public and private, indoor and outdoor meetings a week were held in all parts of Britain, addressed by almost as many speakers. In London alone, some 150 meetings a month were held in 1936, with attendances averaging 1,400.

In February 1937, 222 meetings were held in London. The BUF aimed, as Mosley put it in *The Greater Britain*:

"... to achieve its aim legally and constitutionally, by methods of law and order; but in objective it is revolutionary or it is nothing. It challenges the existing order and advances the constructive alternative of the Corporate State ... It combines the dynamic urge to change and progress, with the authority, the discipline and the order without which nothing great can be achieved."

Seeking power by democratic and constitutional means through the ballot box, the BUF chose 81 parliamentary candidates in 1936. The distribution of selected constituencies gives a good idea of the areas in which we were strong: 39 in London; 16 in Lancashire; 12 in Yorkshire; 6 in the Midlands and 3 in Wales.

Published estimates of the BUF's membership vary from 5,000 to 500,000. I would not be surprised if half a million did join, but this would include people who paid one month's subscription and were never seen or heard of again. A great deal of nonsense has been written on the subject, but though the truth will never be known (for a reason that I will explain) two serious studies have in fact been made.

The first was by the Labour Party in the 1930s. It studied our Plymouth (Sutton) branch in detail and found that this branch alone had a thousand members.

The second was by the Trevelyan Scholarship Project in 1960. This regional study of the BUF in Yorkshire discovered that we had 5,000 members in just that one county, between 1934 - 40.

The only list of members kept at National Headquarters was of those 9,000 or so members who were currently active. From this the Government wrongly concluded that the BUF's total membership was 9,000. Lists of non-active members were held only by individual branches, many of which also had a secret membership consisting of people who could not afford to be publicly associated with us - senior police officers, local government officials, businessmen and civil servants. Records of these secret members were kept neither at Headquarters nor on the branch premises.

The BUF advocated government by experts, and it had many able, experienced and distinguished advisers. Among these were: Major-General MacMunn (Indian Affairs); Captain Robert Gordon-Canning (Foreign Affairs); Major-General J. F. C. Fuller (Military and Defence) and Commander Carlyon Bellairs, R.N. (Naval Affairs).

Gordon-Canning was a descendant of the great 19th Century Prime Minister and Foreign Secretary, George Canning. His special interest was the Arab world, and he had served on the staff of the famous Rif leader, Abd-el-Krim.

Major-General Fuller was one of Britain's two foremost military analysts and historians, the other being Captain Basil Liddell-Hart. In November 1917, as chief general staff officer of the Tank Corps Fuller led the attack at Cambrai in which massed tanks were used for the first time - one of the great turning points in the history of warfare. Between 1919 and 1939 his numerous writings on mechanised warfare were ignored by the British General Staff, carefully studied by the German High Command, and put into successful action by General Guderian.

For Carlyon Bellairs, joining "an emergency group of men and women to advocate a practical policy" for a possible future national crisis was not a new experience. Thirty years earlier he had been asked by Sidney and Beatrice Webb to join their brains trust for national revival. Among the dozen expert members were: Leopold Amery (Military Affairs), Sir Edward Grey (Foreign Policy), Viscount Haldane (The Law), Halford J. Mackinder (whose 1904 paper, "*The Geographical Pivot of History*" influenced the later thinking of the German geopoliticians), Bertrand Russell

(Science), Sidney Webb (Municipal Affairs), and H. G. Wells (Science). What an extraordinarily impressive group! Several of them became real Cabinet Ministers, after their apprenticeship in the Webbs' Cabinet Brains Trust.

The kind of ideas that Sidney and Beatrice Webb had at this time was very different from those they later expressed as uncritical admirers of the Soviet Union. They wanted a government of specialists aiming at National Efficiency, and "racial improvement", which Beatrice Webb called "the most important of all questions, this breeding of the right sort of man."

It is perhaps not so surprising that Commander Carlyon Bellairs became a supporter of our Movement.

We members of the BUF regarded the Labour Party with contempt. In two periods of office it had done nothing to remedy social ills or create prosperity. MacDonald, Webb, Snowden and Thomas had given proof of their unfitness to govern. At the same time, we had considerable respect for some socialists - for people like Tom Mann, Keir Hardie, Ben Tillett, Robert Blatchford and George Lansbury. These men represented "human Socialism". In the case of one of them, Robert Blatchford, we were in almost total agreement, for we too wished to return to a small-scale society, to keep the Englishness of England, and there was little indeed in his book *Merrie England* with which we disagreed. Anyone who compares the contents of Blatchford's weekly *Clarion* in the 1890s with those of our paper *Action* in the 1930s will find interesting parallels - attacks on sweated industries, appeals to patriotism. Even the circulations were similar.

It was the representatives of Marxist "scientific Socialism" whom we abhorred - the Coles, Dutts, Laskis, Stracheys and Webbs. Blatchford himself had realised that there was a different kind of Socialism to the kind he believed in - one that would lead through blood and fire "to a new Utopia where there shall be neither law, nor Government, nor religion", a "godless, graceless, hopeless Commonwealth." What could possibly be regarded as "scientific" about the teachings of a man who considered everything predictable and his own predictions infallible? We believed in solving problems by pragmatic action, that the human condition like the Universe itself was in a constant state of change, and that the arrogant dialectical rigidity of Marxism could only put the human race in a strait-jacket.

As I write this in 1984, with Trotskyist extremists warring with moderates in most of its branches, Mosley's verdict on the Labour Party seems as valid as ever:

"It is part of the fatality of Labour that the leader is always dependent on a balance of forces which inhibit action. The prisoner leader is an invariable result of the whole structure, psychology and character of the party."

Using the slogan "'Gainst Trust and Monopoly", the BUF supported the little man against the big battalions: the small shopkeeper against the cut-price multiples, the independent taxi-driver against the fleet companies, the self-employed craftsman, the street trader, the fisherman, the smallholder, the market gardener. And it believed in other respects that "small is beautiful". It was hostile not only to the dark satanic mills and soulless factories with their thousands of workers but to the very cities that contained them. After all the festering city slums had been destroyed in the military-style operation proposed by Mosley, their inhabitants would be rehoused in small and largely self-sufficient communities, in rural environments.

Such ideas seemed to be swimming against the tide, mere pipe dreams to a society that thought the giant enterprises and mass production methods ushered in by the Industrial Revolution were here to stay. Mosley knew better. Just as human muscle power had given way to mechanical power, requiring reform of the political and social institutions of an agricultural society, so in a process of accelerating change would mechanical power be supplanted in its turn.

Because the new Scientific Revolution was dynamic, because productive capacity would grow at an ever-faster pace while human labour became increasingly superfluous, mere tinkering with the machinery of Government would not be enough. The changes required in society's institutions would have to be revolutionary and the more drastic the longer they were delayed.

As the end of the Twentieth Century approaches, Britain's politicians seem just as incapable of grasping these facts as they were when Mosley first pointed them out in 1930.

Louise Irvine

The Press Photographer

IN THE LATE 1920s and early 1930s it was as difficult to keep a job as it was to get one. After leaving school, I worked first in a Manchester newspaper office and then became a stoker on a tramp steamer, travelling the world. I settled in London for a while and became an active member of the New Party.

My father died in 1932, just before the BUF was founded, and I went back North, where I joined the Manchester branch. In the early Autumn of 1933, the members of our small Stockton-on-Tees branch were having a rough time at the hands of Communists. Individual members were being assaulted and the branch meetings broken up. After our principal northern speaker, Captain Vincent Collier, had been threatened with a lynching, we decided it was time to do something about it. The following week, a picked 100-strong contingent of Blackshirts from Manchester, Teeside and Tyneside assembled in Middlesbrough and marched to Stockton's Market Square, where our local branch was struggling to hold a meeting, faced by a hostile crowd, hundreds strong. As the missiles - bricks and potatoes studded with razor blades - began to descend on us, the Defence Force moved forward like a machine, driving the Reds back 40 yards.

During this fighting, which went on intermittently for several hours, I was hit in the eye by a stone. It was a serious injury. An operation to save the sight of this eye was unsuccessful. Ever since the age of 21 I have been blind in one eye.

Returning to London, I became a freelance photographer, and many of my photographs were published in our Movement's papers. There was a very large demand for photographs of BUF events from the press, overseas as well as at home, and two of our members, Jack Hart and Peter Atkinson, found it profitable to run "The BUF Photo Agency" from Fleet Street.

As soon as I came into contact with other members of the BUF I realised that it possessed a very special kind of élan. New members changed almost visibly. I suppose it was the kind of transformation that takes place in a rookie after he enters a crack regiment.

What Mosley instilled in his followers was a new spirit of pride - pride in self and country. He himself expressed it as follows: "Our creed and our movement instil in man the heroic attitude to life, because he needs heroism. Our new Britons require the virility of the Elizabethan combined with the intellect and method of the modern technician" (*Tomorrow We Live*). "Deliberately we willed the birth of a type who was half soldier and half politician, partly a tough warrior . . . and partly an inspired idealist . . . This was our dream . . . and in many fine young men it was largely realised." (*My Life*).

This new proud attitude to life, this ardour, this dash, this vivacity, was described by Mosley as panache, a word that seems entirely appropriate in both its senses.

Much has been said and written about the International Brigade. Many of our most violent opponents joined the "Clement Attlee" battalion and hundreds of them were killed between November 1936 and September 1938. Hardly anything is heard of those Britons who fought in the Spanish Nationalist cause. One such was Peter Keen, a member of our Streatham branch and a good friend of mine. He fought for Franco and was awarded a medal. When the Russians attacked Finland in November 1939, Peter joined the international force of volunteers raised to help the Finns. At the end of the unequal 3-month war, in which Finland put up a surprisingly strong defence, the Russians broke through the Mannerheim Line and the Volunteers retreated into Sweden where most of them were interned. Back in England, Peter joined the Airborne Division and served in its Intelligence Section. Peter wore the ribbon of his Franco decoration on his tunic. One day his commanding officer admonished him for doing this, but Peter won the argument by quoting one section of King's Regulations that said all decorations must be worn and another that enjoined officers to "interpret regulations reasonably and intelligently". After 1945 he became a theatre agent and in the 1950s was killed in a car accident.

I took part in the London County Council elections of 1937, in which our candidates won 18 per cent of the votes - despite the fact that the municipal vote was limited to ratepayers (generally the heads of families) and our young supporters were not enfranchised.

The national press grudgingly admitted that we had done well. "The size of their vote was a surprise even to those in touch with the East End", said *The Observer.* "The results gained . . . are rather surprising indications ... of the strength attained in some working-class districts" reported the Manchester Guardian. "A disturbing feature of the elections is the large number of votes recorded" complained the Communist *Daily Worker*.

On election night, I, together with hundreds of other BUF supporters, waited outside Shoreditch Town Hall to hear the result of the count. The police had separated the factions - Mosley supporters on one side of the street and Labour and Communists on the other. When the Communists raised the red flag with its yellow hammer and sickle, fighting began, and the "people's flag" disappeared in the melee. I was arrested and deposited in the police station opposite the Town Hall. In my cell, I played cards for several hours with my jailers before being released without any charge against me.

In April 1937 when the Spanish Civil War was raging, the

Labour Party organised a large rally in Hyde Park to 'Save Spain'. I went along to this meeting and noticed that about twenty yards from where Sir Stafford Cripps was speaking a tall blonde girl of proud bearing was being menaced by a section of the crowd. Guessing that she might be one of us I barged my way to her side, arriving there at the same time as a solitary policeman. Kicked and punched, the three of us made our way towards Marble Arch, where, helped by two more policemen, we jumped on a bus, narrowly escaping several hundred pursuers. After a short ride along Oxford Street we got off the bus and stopped for tea in a restaurant. A week later, to my great surprise, I received a return invitation to tea at the home of her parents, Lord and Lady Redesdale. The girl was, of course, Unity Mitford, who had infuriated the English admirers of the Spanish churchburners by wearing an NSDAP badge. A small group of BUF members who had also attended this Red rally and bravely if foolhardily given the Fascist salute were less lucky. Fierce fighting broke out, and two of them, George Curzon and Eric Steer, ended up as patients in St. George's Hospital.

In 1937, on my way to visit our Summer Camp in Sussex, I stopped at a small country hotel for lunch and to my surprise found Mosley lunching there with Neil Francis-Hawkins, our second-in-command. Mosley invited me to join them. It was my first personal meeting with him.

Mosley too was on his way to the camp, and on arriving there found a surprise gift awaiting him. It was an M.G. car, bought with the proceeds of a collection of 'pennies and pounds' and intended to replace his aging Bentley. It was presented by South Coast Inspector Peter Symes who wished him "thousands of miles of mechanically trouble-free journeying." Mosley was so deeply touched that for the first and last time in his life found difficulty in finding the words to express his thanks.

Carping criticism of the police is a much-used Communist ploy for subverting the existing social order. An experience I had with the National Council for Civil Liberties is illuminating. The NCCL, with its office at the time in the Communist Party's national headquarters, hardly bothered to conceal its affinities.

While covering a BUF meeting at which there was some fighting I photographed a policeman bending over a member of the opposition who was prostate on the ground. This man was arrested, and so was I, and we both had to appear at Bow Street Court. Within 48 hours, I received a letter from the indefatigable Ronald Kidd, secretary of the NCCL, stating that the other defendant had informed him of my arrest and that as a press photographer I might think that the police had "taken this case against you vindictively." Ronald Kidd, ignorant of my politics, was hoping to make a complaint against the police. When I told him I had taken this photograph for *Action* his interest in this 'injustice' ended abruptly. The only civil liberties that the NCCL has ever been interested in preserving are those of Leftists.

Then came the war. In the summer of 1940 the Special Branch had a detention order to deliver to one of *Action's* photographers but I managed to evade them. I joined the Pioneer Corps, saw action in Belgium and Holland, was commissioned with my Commanding Officer's full knowledge of my BUF past, and was mentioned in despatches.

In the final weeks of the war I was one of a number of British officers chosen for a special secret mission in Northern Germany - to organise German units who had surrendered in good shape to fight alongside the British and Americans, should the Soviet forces advance too far west!

On 4th July 1977, I read of the Israeli airborne commando raid to rescue 103 mostly Jewish hostages held by a PLO group aboard an Air France plane at Entebbe Airport, Uganda. Jews in Uganda? This rang a bell, and suddenly I remembered. Forty years earlier, a Government Committee presided over by Lord Peel had produced a report advocating the division of Palestine into Arab and Jewish states. A BUF study group came up with its own suggestion, and this was announced in a lecture entitled "A Jewish Homeland: Where?" given by one of our principal speakers, Clement Bruning. Our study group proposed the creation of not one Jewish state but two. The Palestinian state would consist of a 3,000 square mile coastal strip extending from the Egyptian border to that of the Lebanon. A corridor would lead to Jerusalem, which would be an autonomous city. A second Jewish state would be established in Uganda, which was lightly populated and nearly ten times the size of Palestine. Countries with large Jewish populations - Poland, Germany, France, Britain and the United States - would provide the funds to purchase land. This plan (not likely to have met with the approval of our Foreign Policy Adviser, Robert Gordon-Canning!) did not become official party policy. But it was one of many constructive proposals: the BUF buzzed with imaginative ideas for dealing with a great variety of problems. One scheme for providing work for the unemployed involved the reclamation of The Wash.

Uganda had been suggested by Joseph Chamberlain at the beginning of the century, but had been rejected at three Zionist conferences. Was our scheme to establish two National Homes for the Jews impractical? The Government's own scheme was rejected on the grounds of its "impracticality". It is ironic that a plan that should have appealed to a great many Jews was probably responsible for the legend that "Mosley wants to expel all Jews from Britain."

It is both ironic and poignant that Clement Bruning, who announced our plan, perished during the War - in a German prison camp. My admiration for Mosley remains as strong as ever. Into the sordid, self-seeking world of party politics he brought integrity and quality. England will never again see the like of its Lost Hero.

John Warburton

The Welsh Security Officer

I WAS BORN in Cardiff in the first year of the Twentieth Century, son of a Welsh father and a Spanish mother. My father was an enthusiastic Socialist and early Fabian and many leading politicians such as Ramsay Macdonald and Philip Snowden and his wife Ethel stayed in our home. At that time, Snowden was, I think, chairman of the Independent Labour Party. Later as Chancellor of the Exchequer in the Labour Governments of 1924 and 1929-31 Snowden, as a completely orthodox economist, was the chief opponent of that most unorthodox economist, Oswald Mosley.

Like so many people with Welsh blood in their veins I had a good singing voice. One day, at my father's prompting I gave a solo performance in church. The song chosen happened to be a well-known hymn tune, but the words were Jim Connell's The Red Flag. In those days church-going Liberals and Conservatives regarded Socialists with the same horror as Socialists later regarded Fascists, and this incident caused such a scandal that it reached the ears of the Bishop, who promptly refused to confirm me. And unconfirmed I remain, at the age of 85.

Following my Army service during and after the First World War, I arrived in London in search of work. In 1933 I joined the Central London branch of the BUF, with rather splendid offices in Curzon Street, Mayfair. Most of the members of this branch were titled people or high-ranking serving and retired army and navy officers. Some were both. The wearing of the black shirt certainly helped to conceal the social differences. I was soon invited to become a member of the special defence Force better known as the "I" Squad, the members of which were distinguished from others by wearing breeches. The "I" Squad was divided into four units of nine men, and was under the command of Eric Hamilton Piercy.

At the same time that he ran the "I" Squad, Piercy was also an Inspector of Special Constabulary. His second-in-command was Arthur Mills. According to our opponents, our task was to beat up anyone who dared to ask a question at a Mosley meeting. A moment's reflection reveals the absurdity of this. In reality, the Communists tried to smash our meetings by organised barracking and violence, and we threw them out after they had been given three clear warnings by the speaker. Ejecting a large group of them naturally involved a fierce free for all, but though we never started these fights we always finished them successfully.

The joke was that so many on our side came from the same kind of Socialistic background as our most deadly enemies. They regarded us as "the last resort of reactionary capitalism in decline" - the defenders of capitalist society, when in fact we were proposing a third way between Marxism and liberalism. The great divide in our respective beliefs concerned the nature of Marxism and of the Soviet Union. We totally rejected Marx and Engels' claim in *The Communist Manifesto* that "... communism abolishes eternal truths; it abolishes all religion, and all morality, instead of constituting them on a new basis. It therefore acts in contradiction to all past historical experience." We also realised that a society based on such beliefs would always feel threatened by the existence anywhere in the world of any other kind of society. In contrast to the preposterous teaching that all pre-Marxist philosophical ideas were fantasies our beliefs were based on a simple rational concept - the "union of opposites":

". . . synthesis of the Christian conception of service, self-abnegation, self-sacrifice in the cause of others . . . with the Nietzschean conception of virility, the challenge to everything that impedes the forward march of man, absolute abnegation of the doctrine of surrender: the firm ability to grapple with and to overcome all obstructions." In practical terms, we wanted a scientifically-managed society under efficient leadership, in which expert executives replaced amateur legislators and a united people had a common purpose.

"If Mosley is a revolutionary, why does he always promptly obey a police instruction to end a rowdy meeting or march?" people used to ask. The answer is that Mosley was a revolutionary in that he wanted to change the way society is organised; he was a strict constitutionalist with the greatest respect for the law; he did not advocate violent revolution. In his 1932 book *The Greater Britain* he wrote:

"Fascism is the greatest constructive and revolutionary creed in the world. It seeks to achieve its aim legally and constitutionally, by methods of law and order; but in objective it is revolutionary or it is nothing. It challenges the existing order and advances the constructive alternative of the Corporate State ... It combines the dynamic urge to change and progress, with the authority, the discipline and the order without which nothing great can be achieved." But at a time when a bloody Communist revolution seemed quite possible, Mosley also wrote:

"In the final economic crisis to which neglect may lead, argument, reason, persuasion vanish and organised force alone prevails. In such a situation, the eternal protagonists in the history of all modern crises must struggle for the mastery of the State."

The BUF was organised as an army to meet this threat, which seemed perfectly natural to its members, most of us being ex-Servicemen anyway. Mosley drew a parallel with the New Model Army of Fairfax and Cromwell, and the BUF with twenty thousand disciplined members represented a force quite equal to Cromwell's - and a great deal more experienced in war.

From secret documents now released to the Public Record Office, it is obvious that the National Government of Baldwin and

Chamberlain did not believe that the purpose of our military-type organisation was to oppose a Communist revolution. It regarded the BUF as likely to seize power by force. We were treated with the greatest suspicion throughout our existence by the Government, while those who constituted the real threat to Western Civilisation were not merely tolerated but cosseted.

Next to the Communists, the members of the Independent Labour Party - the Militant Tendency of the 1930s - were probably our most violent opponents, yet strangely enough many of our best recruits had come from the ILP: Henry J. Gibbs, W. J. Leaper, editor of our paper, and John Scanlon, author of The Decline and Fall of the Labour Party. Between Mosley and Maxton, the ILP leader, there was a lifelong personal affection and regard - as there was, surprisingly, between Mosley and Michael Foot.

There were many remarkable personalities in the BUF, including at least seven clergymen: the Revs. H. E. B. Nye, E. C. Opie, A. Palmer, Ellis Roberts, Thomas, Tibbs and Yate-Allen. Several captains of ocean-going liners were members, such as Captain Mott of the Cunard Line.

Joe Beckett the boxer, and his very strong-willed wife were also enthusiastic members. They belonged to our Southampton branch. Joe gained his first important boxing victories in 1914, and by defeating Bombardier Billy Wells on 27th February 1919 became the English heavyweight champion. After being twice defeated by George Carpentier, Joe retired from the ring.

Others I remember particularly are: W. G. Barlow, ex-Royal Flying Corps pilot and racing motorist; Dick Plathen, our first Meetings Organiser; George Sutton, Mosley's secretary from Labour Party days on; the shy and gentle Ernie D. Hart, in charge of National Headquarters Research; and three senior naval officers: Commander Aitkin, R.N. - whose son Max was a fellow member of the "I" Squad; Commander Charles Hudson, R.N.; and Vice-Admiral G. B. Powell, who was organiser of our

Portsmouth branch. But it was for two army men that I held a particular esteem: the Hamers, father and son. Lieutenant-Colonel Frederick Hamer had joined the Royal Marines in 1903 and served throughout the First World War, while his son, Richard, had been commissioned firstly in the Royal Tank Corps and then in the South Wales Borderers.

A quite incredible number of people joined the BUF during the first two years of its existence, when it received extensive publicity. Some of the *Daily Mail's* readers switched from the rather staid local Conservative Club to this exciting new party. Branches began to resemble Conservative clubs, for such members were only interested in social activities, not in taking our message onto the streets. Eventually, dozens of branches, often with hundreds of members, that had become nothing more than social clubs were closed down.

These people were a pest but we had worse problems with various petty crooks and confidence tricksters who had come in with the flood of recruits. When rumours of the disappearing funds of one particular branch reached the Top Brass I was sent as a kind of undercover agent to investigate carefully. I took lodgings in the district and joined the branch in the guise of a new local recruit, and began to collect evidence discreetly. It soon became apparent that the branch organiser and the treasurer were pocketing most of the subscriptions and donations. I duly made my report to National Headquarters and the offending officials were promptly expelled from the Movement. To my surprise I was thereupon asked to take over control of that particular branch. This I did, and in 1936 I was selected to be our Movement's prospective Parliamentary candidate for the constituency.

From 1935 to 1940 I remained branch organiser, devoting seven evenings a week to my task, until it all came to an end so abruptly and sadly in the late Spring of the first year of the War.

Arthur Beavan

The Norfolk Bailiff

I FIRST HEARD of Mosley in 1931 in rather unusual circumstances. I was returning to England from the South Seas on a French ship, Ville de Verdun, and just as we entered the northern hemisphere the wireless operator picked up a news item: "In England Sir Oswald Mosley has formed a New Party."

After eight years abroad, the conditions I found at home shocked me. The Labour Party had been in power for two years yet unemployment had swollen to 2½ millions. When at the beginning of October 1932 Mosley launched the British Union of Fascists I was immediately interested but felt wary about actually joining because I had read in the *Morning Post* that the BUF's appeal was almost exclusively to the upper classes!

In the Spring of 1933 I decided to apply for membership, and in consequence received a visit at my home in Norfolk from the very first Blackshirt I had ever seen. I was immediately impressed by the personal charm and eloquence of this tall, good-looking man.

G. S. Gerault's great-grandfather had fled from France during the French Revolution, while Gerault himself was a schoolmaster who had served as an officer in the First World War. The main argument that he put to me was that the BUF's policy combined the patriotism of the Right with the social reforms of the Left. It was the message I had been waiting for. I joined.

The first time I saw Mosley and heard him speak was at a crowded meeting at the Corn Hall, King's Lynn on a Saturday afternoon some months later. I have never forgotten what he said on that occasion. He explained how the machinery of government was hopelessly out-of-date in the age of the internal combustion engine and the aeroplane, and why it needed to be drastically overhauled to bring it in line with the enormous scientific advances of the past century. He spelt out to his largely farming audience just how their livelihoods were being threatened by cheap dumped imported foodstuffs, and how he would give the British farmer first place in the British market, the farmers of the Empire second place, and foreign farmers little or none.

Among those who joined at the end of the meeting - dozens did at the end of almost every meeting that Mosley addressed - was Dorothy, Viscountess Downe, a neighbour, former Lady-in-Waiting and close personal friend of Queen Mary. She remained a courageous and loyal supporter of Mosley and the BUF throughout the persecution of the war-years right up to her death in 1958.

During the "Tithe War", described in detail in an earlier chapter, Douglas Gunson who farmed in north-east Norfolk and I were the only two BUF officials in the area not incarcerated.

In 1935 I was summoned to our new National Headquarters in Sanctuary Buildings, Great Smith Street, Westminster, to attend my first conference of senior officials. This was the first time I met Mosley in council, though I had seen him many times on the platform and in relaxed conversation with followers and admirers after meetings.

A new facet of his character was revealed to me on this occasion - his extraordinary ability to probe directly to the root of a problem. One question after another was laid before him which we, his lieutenants, had found insoluble. As each knotty problem was presented to him he would reflect in silence for a moment. Then he would lean forward across the table looking directly at whoever had posed the question and propound his remedy. It was an exhibition of exceptional mental ability and speed of perception.

In a flash the problem would be clarified, reduced to basics, and a sound remedy proposed. No wonder Harold Macmillan described Mosley as the most able man he had ever met.

Following Anthony Eden's visit to Rome in the summer of 1935, which caused intense bitterness there, Italy invaded Abyssinia. Mosley thereupon launched the "Mind Britain's Business" campaign, and hundreds of meetings were held throughout the country. During this period he himself addressed three or four meetings a week.

This vigorous campaign against Sanctions and the danger of war resulted in a noticeable improvement in the general public's attitude to our Movement. The people of Britain were not willing to go to war for the sake of "The Lion of Judah". The BUF's speakers suddenly became aware that a great many more fair-minded people were listening to them.

For the first time Mosley addressed vast, enthusiastic audiences in East London. He spoke to a crowd of 100,000 people in Victoria Park, Bethnal Green, and to an audience of 10,000 in the market place in Norwich - his biggest open-air meeting in the provinces up to that time.

I regard the time from the Abyssinian War (1935) until Churchill's appointment as Prime Minister (1940) as the period in the BUF's history to which it is possible to look back with the greatest pride. The easy optimism of the early days had been replaced by sober determination and stern resolve. We could now see that we were in for a long, hard and dangerous struggle. There was no quick timetable for victory: only the certainty that unless Mosley prevailed, the sun would set forever on Britain and on her imperial glory.

At the outset of the Abdication Crisis of 1936, Mosley declared that he stood firm for the King. The BUF launched a great propaganda drive, "Stand By The King", and this slogan was printed on thousands of leaflets and whitewashed on hundreds of walls. We also issued a special news-sheet, *Crisis*, which every available member sold on the street. I was living in Manchester at the time and my very first customer was Sir Henry Wood, returning home from a rehearsal of the Halle Orchestra.

During this period I was responsible for organising all our Movement's meetings in a vast area stretching from Birmingham to Newcastle. With reports coming in to me all the time, I was in a better position than most to assess the reaction of Midlanders and Northerners to the Crisis. The middle classes generally regarded the proposed morganatic marriage (by which Mrs. Simpson would be Edward's wife but not Queen) as an affront to petit bourgeois respectability and considered that Edward should abdicate. The working classes, on the other hand, apart from the Marxist Left, were solidly for the King. They knew he sympathised with their plight, and remembered the promise he made to the unemployed miners of South Wales when he visited the distressed areas: "Something will be done".

On 11th December, 1936, came the news that Edward had abdicated, and thus ended the brief reign of the most popular King who ever succeeded to the Throne of England. It is fitting that after 1955, as near neighbours on the outskirts of Paris, these two men, rejected by the Establishment of England, became close friends.

Among many outstanding meetings I recall one in the coal-mining town of Barnsley in Yorkshire. The meeting began ominously as our Colours were booed when the Barnsley branch members paraded them down the aisle. Then when Mosley appeared on the platform there was an angry howl, and it was some minutes before he could begin his speech. But soon the assembled miners were listening with close attention as Mosley spoke of the iniquity of allowing vast quantities of Polish coal into Britain at a time when tens of thousands of our miners were unemployed. He said that the extraction of petroleum from coal could prove a great boost to the industry but the process was being held up in the interests of the great oil companies. Beginning badly, this meeting ended triumphantly, even though a stone-throwing Communist mob waited outside.

In 1936, Parliament passed the Public Order Act. This Act was directed not against the Communist perpetrators of violence but at those at the receiving end, i.e. the BUF. We did not try to break up their meetings, as they did ours. The Morning Post wrote of the Blackshirts at this time:

"They are loyal to King and Country. They never assault the police and, except when attacked by hooligans, do not resort to the gentle laying on of hands ... it is difficult to understand why the leaders of the so-called Labour Party condone the lawlessness of an East End mob, while furiously demanding the suppression of a handful of law-abiding fascists."

The Leftwing organisations and newspapers which had enthusiastically supported this Bill when it was directed against us were highly indignant when, after the Second World War, there was talk of using it to curtail the activities of CND.

When an acute financial crisis hit the BUF in 1937, 101 out of a total National Headquarters staff of 140 had to be dismissed; the NHQ offices were reduced by two-thirds in size; and the Northern Headquarters in Corporation Street, Manchester closed. It says much for the men and women concerned that, with four exceptions, they remained unshaken in their loyalty. These drastic economies resulted in a speeding up of the decentralisation that was already under way, senior local officials assuming most of the former administrative functions of NHQ.

I doubt if any political leader or party in Britain has ever encountered such dishonourable treatment and unreasoning prejudice as Mosley and his Movement. Throughout the 1930s, the ceaseless denigration, misrepresentation and barefaced lying by the press, BBC and public men poisoned the minds of many otherwise reasonable citizens.

A story told by Doreen Bell, one of our youngest and most able speakers, is relevant and revealing. Travelling by train in a compartment with a Nonconformist minister she got into conversation with him. They discussed the sad state of Britain and Miss Bell outlined Mosley's policy for reviving British agriculture and industry. Her listener expressed warm and total agreement with all she had said. Arriving at her destination Miss Bell rose and said: "Those are the policies advocated by Mosley." The clergyman looked shocked. "If I had known that, I would never have agreed with anything that you have told me."

After 1937, defamatory press attacks on us were replaced by a campaign of total silence. Mosley addressed enthusiastic meetings all over Britain attended by many thousands of people, but the national newspapers made no mention of these meetings or of what he said at them. Thenceforth our meetings only received some brief mention if violence occurred at them - violence initiated as always by the extreme Left.

Because there was little or no mention of the BUF in the press from 1937 to 1940, many modern historians concluded that our Movement must have been on the wane in this period. Fortunately this misleading impression has since been corrected by Professor Robert Skidelsky and others.

In one month alone, Mosley addressed audiences of nearly half a million people, yet not a word was reported in the national press. As the Editor of *The Aeroplane* put it at the time:

"One may dislike Sir Oswald Mosley. But a press which ignores meetings at which audiences amount to many, many thousands at a time, and are moved to great enthusiasm, cannot profess to be a representative press . . . The great danger of such suppression of truth and suggestion of falsehood, is that we may be driven into a war in which we are not concerned, and in the interests of alien political movements and international finance."

In November 1937, the National Association of Wholesale Newsagents suddenly refused to handle *Action*, which until then had been on sale in most newsagents' shops in the country, and had the largest sale of any political weekly - much larger than the *New Statesman* or the *Spectator*. This was a crippling blow to us. So much for the much-vaunted "Freedom of the Press".

During the Spanish Civil War, as during the Italian-Abyssinian War, Mosley was adamant that Britain should not become involved, although his sympathies were wholly with the Spanish Nationalists. He even forbade his followers to fight for Franco. This may seem a surprisingly insular attitude, but British Fascism was an intensely national creed, something our opponents have never been able to understand.

Our consistent demands for peace brought increased membership and growing respect, up to and beyond the outbreak of war. With halls denied to us and public parks and loudspeakers forbidden by Labour-controlled councils, we held marches instead - from the Victoria Embankment or Millbank to Bermondsey, Ridley Road, Dalston and Trafalgar Square. The number of marchers increased by thousands. To encourage the immensely long columns were a number of bands, drum and trumpet, drum and pipe, drum and bugle. The women's contingent was led by its own drum corps. In the centre of the huge parade were our massed standards - the red, white and blue of Union Jacks and the black and gold of the branches' insignia, all carried by ex-Servicemen whose chests were covered with campaign medals and decorations.

In my work for our Movement in the North of England I witnessed the collapse of the cotton industry in Lancashire under the competition of Asian mills. A skilled worker in an Indian cotton mill earned 15p a day. How could Lancashire compete with this

? The Labour Party had no remedy except nationalisation. The Conservatives advocated rationalisation, which meant scrapping spindles and sacking workers. The BUF's policy was to exclude all Asian cloth from Britain and the Colonial Empire and to adopt a general trading policy of "Britain Buys from Those who Buy from Britain". These sensible proposals were received enthusiastically by many in the cotton trade, and our Movement expanded rapidly throughout Lancashire.

The BUF branches in Blackburn and Nelson were typical of dozens more. Bill Sumner was the branch organiser in Blackburn, that archetypal cotton town. He was an ex-Regular corporal of cavalry, whose rasping voice would be heard in the market place every Wednesday. While Sumner and his large family subsisted with the meagre aid of the Public Assistance Board, the local women's organiser was the daughter of a well-to-do landowning family. The branch treasurer, Jack Birtwistle, was a young carpenter, while most of the members were unemployed millhands and mechanics.

Further north in Nelson, the dominant branch official was the women's organiser, Nellie Driver, one of the BUF's outstanding personalities in the whole county. Outwardly shy, Nellie was extremely strong-minded and zealous, and she wrote beautiful poetry and prose. Our Movement had no more devoted apostles than Nellie Driver and her mother, and they made many converts.

Our most important meeting of 1937 took place shortly before Christmas, in the Free Trade Hall, Manchester. Inside, every one of the 3,000 seats was occupied, while thousands more listened through loudspeakers outside in Peter Street. On this occasion Mosley's speech was devoted largely to foreign affairs. He warned of the growing danger of war, and called on his audience to help him establish Britain once more as a world leader and keeper of world peace.

On 9th July, 193, Mosley initiated the "Britain First" campaign with meetings, rallies and marches throughout the length and breadth of the country. Two million anti-war leaflets were delivered to homes. The climax to this campaign was a meeting in Stonlake Road, Hammersmith on the last Sunday in September - also the BUF's 6th anniversary - a meeting attended by a huge audience.

When Neville Chamberlain gave Poland a carte blanche guarantee on 30th March, 1939, Mosley almost alone among public figures in Britain realised the grave dangers involved - realised that Chamberlain by this reckless act might be signing away Britain's greatness and dooming her Empire to extinction.

On Sunday, 7th May, 1939, the BUF made its greatest-ever show of strength with a march from Westminster to Hackney. Standing shoulder to shoulder in three ranks, the marchers extended from Westminster along the Embankment to Hungerford Bridge.

Mosley's meeting at Earl's Court on Sunday, 16th July, 1939, at which he addressed an audience estimated to number 30,000, was the largest indoor meeting of any kind held anywhere in the world. It marked the peak of our Movement's strength and influence. I found myself sitting next to an admiral who had motored up from Plymouth. Parties and individuals came from as far as Edinburgh and Dundee. The London Passenger Transport Board put on special through-trains on the Underground, to bring in thousands of members and supporters from East London. After Mosley mounted the huge rostrum, it was several minutes before his cheering, waving and saluting audience would let him speak. Most of his speech was devoted to a passionate plea for peace.

All our meetings and marches for peace during that summer were in vain. On 1st September, 1939 the German Army crossed the Polish frontier and on 3rd September Britain declared war on Germany. Many of our members were already serving in the armed forces, and especially in the Royal Air Force. Within 24 hours of the declaration of war two of our finest members, K. G. Day and G. T. Brocking, were killed in Number 107 Squadron's raid on the Kiel Canal in which several German warships were damaged. Another member, a pilot, got back safely from this raid, though badly wounded, to be rewarded by detention under Defence Regulation 18B the following summer. Thus it was that the names of BUF members appeared in the RAF's very first casualty list of the war.

On 1st September Mosley issued the following instruction to all BUF members and supporters:

"Our country is involved in war. Therefore I ask you to do nothing to injure our country, or to help any other power. Our members should do what the law requires of them; and, if they are members of any of the Forces or Services of the Crown, they should obey their orders, and, in every particular, obey the rules of their Service."

A similar statement was issued on 14th March, 1940. On Sunday, 5th May, 1940 we held seventeen meetings in East London before Mosley spoke to an audience of tens of thousands in Victoria Park Square, Bethnal Green, in the evening. There our Colours and massed Standards were paraded for what was to be the last time.

Our newspaper *Action* subsequently reported:

"After a mighty rendering of the National Anthem, it was some minutes before the audience would allow Mosley to leave . . . Thus ended the greatest day that British Union had yet witnessed".

Five days later Hitler launched his Blitzkrieg in the West, Churchill succeeded Chamberlain as Prime Minister and - most ominously for us - seven Labour leaders were invited to join the Coalition Government. These men, nearly all of whom had been pacifists and conscientious objectors during the First

World War, proved to be the most bellicose members of the Government. We have it on the word of a well-known Labour parliamentary candidate, Hugh Ross Williamson, that the arrest and imprisonment of Mosley and his followers had been one of their conditions for entering the Government.

Shortly before the outbreak of war I had moved from the North of England to Canterbury to help organise that Parliamentary division for Lady Pearson, who was to contest that seat for us in the General Election due to take place that autumn. Due to the outbreak of war, no General Election took place, but I remained in Canterbury as branch organiser. On 14th May, 1940 the German armoured divisions broke through the 9th French Army at Sedan and a broadcast appeal went out to all men between 17 and 60 to join the Local Defence Volunteers (later called the Home Guard). I enrolled immediately, and on my first patrol was posted to the top of a Down where the flames of Dunkirk were visible and the sounds of gunfire and explosions could be heard.

Visiting the Royal Army Service Corps Supply Office in Canterbury a day or two later in the course of my work, I met Colonel Gabriel, R.A.S.C., and as I never concealed my political views I told him I was a member of Mosley's Movement.

"Then", said the colonel, "you cannot possibly know what I know about that organisation. Are you aware that the local fascist leader has a safe-conduct signed personally by Hitler instructing the German military authorities to spare this man and his household?"

"Are you quite sure of your facts?" I asked.

"I received that information from an absolutely reliable source ', Colonel Gabriel replied.

It would be an understatement to say that he looked disconcerted when I told him that I was the "local fascist leader". Such was the kind of hysterical and absurd rumour spread by normally responsible people in the invasion panic of the time.

On 22nd May, Defence Regulation 18B was amended for the specific purpose of incarcerating Mosley and his followers. The centuries-old safeguard against arbitrary imprisonment, Habeas Corpus, was suspended in order to settle old scores by a piece of vindictive, retrospective legislation. The next day, as Mosley arrived by car at his flat in Dolphin Square, Westminster, at 3.30 p.m. he was "detained" under an order the existence of which he was unaware and the terms of which he had yet to discover.

Among many blackshirts with distinguished war records detained on that day were Major H. de Laessoe, D.S.O., M.C, and Captain U. A. Hick, both of whom had served in the Boer War and the First World War (Hick having lost an arm), Captain Robert Gordon Canning, M.C., an ex-Regular soldier who had served in the 10th Hussars, Captain B.D.E. Donovan, M.C. formerly of the Indian Army, and two ex-pilots who had served in the Royal Flying Corps as well as the Royal Air Force. The men thrown into Brixton Gaol on that day, without charge or trial then or after, had more war wounds, campaign medals and military decorations than the entire British War Cabinet.

The outbreak of the war and the failure to negotiate an honourable peace while that was still possible spelt the end of our greatest hopes. Yet as a second millennium approaches, those few of us who survive can still recall with wonder the Spirit of the BUF - the feelings of adventure, comradeship, dedication and romance during those exciting days of struggle - feelings we would never again recapture during the rest of our lives.

R. R. Bellamy

Afterword

Britain's "Long, Slow Crumbling"

FOR OVER A CENTURY, Britain had grown and prospered through a laissez-faire policy of unrestricted competition and minimal interference with industry. She supplied the rest of the world with her manufactured goods and imported half her food and most of the raw materials needed by industry, except coal.

In 1914, Britain was at the height of her political, military and economic power. The British Empire covered a fifth of the world's area, nearly 14 million square miles, and had a population of over 500 million. British merchant ships transported the world's goods, while the Royal Navy, equal to the combined navies of France and Russia, was by far the most powerful, and controlled the world's oceans. Coal, which had made the Industrial Revolution possible, employed 1¼ million men, and output had reached 287 million tons per annum, of which 73 million tons were exported. Pig iron and steel, the other indicators of industrial power, reached outputs of over 10 million tons and 7¾ million tons. Within the British Isles, over 523 million tons of freight were carried by a railway network of 24,000 miles.

But already there were ominous indications that all was not well with the competitive market economy. After 1873, the rate of growth of Britain's economy had slowed considerably, and the period of falling prices that lasted until 1896 gave rise to Britain's first Great Depression. The causes of this decline sound familiar to us: ageing staple industries, failure to develop new industries; inadequate managements; lack of technical training;

too much investment overseas and too little in Britain; and above all, rapidly increasing competition from newly-industrialised countries, both in Europe and the East.

Despite the cost in blood and money, Britain emerged from the War stronger than she entered it. It was not so in 1945.

For Britain, the economic price of victory in the Second World War was enormous. She had entered the war as a creditor nation and came out of it a debtor. Her overseas assets had been sold to pay for the war and the country was close to bankruptcy. The moment the war with Japan ended, the United States put "business" first, by cutting off Lease-Lend, which alone had made it possible for Britain to fight on for so long. Unable to pay for food and raw materials, Britain had to obtain a loan of £3,750 billion from the United States on humiliating terms in order to avoid economic collapse. This loan was supposed to last until 1951, but was spent in about two years by the admittedly hard-pressed Labour Government. The capital of the loan was added to national indebtedness, bedevilling the nation's financial position for decades.

Nowhere was British weakness shown more clearly than in rationing of essentials. This continued long after the war itself: clothes rationing until March 1949, points rationing until May 1950, soap rationing until September 1950, sweets rationing until February 1953. Britain suffered eight years of rationing during peace after six years of rationing during the war itself - due largely to Labour's obsession, as in 1930, with exports.

The clearest evidence of severely reduced circumstances was the introduction of bread rationing in 1947, which had been avoided throughout the war.

The electorate's revulsion against Churchill's "blood, sweat, toil and tears" swept away the Coalition and put a Labour government into power for six years, and with it the era of rampant state bureaucracy, accelerating inflation and wholesale nationalisation. At a time when Britain needed a rapid recovery above all to face the remainder of the 20th Century, it chose to elect a government obsessed with outdated 19th Century dogma. The present state of coal, steel, shipbuilding and the railways is testimony to that ill-starred experiment in "public ownership."

Historian A. J. P. Taylor gave his own dismal accounting for the war in *English History: 1914/45*:

"The legacy of the war seemed almost beyond bearing . . . Great Britain was in debt to the rest of the world to the extent of £4,198 million. The British merchant marine was 30 per cent smaller than it had been at the beginning of the war. Exports were little more than 40 per cent of the pre-war figure. Government expenditure abroad was five times as great as pre-war . . . Something like 10 per cent of our national wealth had been destroyed, some by physical destruction, the rest by running down our capital assets".

Abroad, the situation was dangerous indeed. The war began as a fight between the fascist states and the democracies, but ended with Soviet communism as the clear gainer, and even more so in the early post-war years. Like a genie escaping from the Russian bottle it spread across Asia, engulfing China in 1949, caused a war in Korea in 1950, and then spread into South-East Asia, over-running Vietnam and what is now Kampuchea, bringing great slaughter with it.

The Red Army had occupied all Europe to the east of Churchill's "iron curtain", and now it blockaded Berlin, to be defeated with difficulty by the airlift mounted by America, Britain and France. Churchill was so alarmed that he made four major speeches between 1948 and 1955, warning that "only the atom bomb in America's possession" prevented the Red Army "subjugating all of Western Europe as far as the Atlantic Ocean". Yet this situation had only arisen through his own ruthless crushing of Germany.

Throughout Europe strong communist parties arose in the chaotic aftermath of the war and at one point seemed about to take power in France and Italy. Communist leaders like Thorez and Togliatti stated openly that in the event of a clash with Russia they would support Russia. In Britain, that faithful running-dog of the red revolution, Harry Pollitt, gave notice that he would play the traitor too.

Alarmed by the potentially disastrous situation in Europe, America stepped in. The new practical-minded President, Harry Truman put General Marshall in charge of a giant rehabilitation programme directed "against hunger, poverty, desperation, and chaos." The Foreign Assistance Act of April 1948 made available $5,300 billion, the bulk to be spent on American goods and raw materials by the participating European nations, and The Organisation for European Economic Cooperation was set up by those nations the same month. Of this sum, Britain received $1,263 billion.

As the economic wheels began to turn again, the communist threat to Western Europe diminished. Even in Britain, hampered by Labour's mass of controls and restrictions, there was a slow industrial recovery. Britain's recovery could have been much more rapid. There were certain factors in our favour then which do not exist today. As Marshall Aid provided the stimulus, opportunities presented themselves in recapturing markets; Britain's industries were relatively unscathed by wartime bombing; trade rivals like Germany and Japan were all-but knocked out.

Once Marshall Aid had done its work, the so-called "Keynesian revolution" was at hand, leading to that "golden age" of thirty years of expanding world trade whose end is so lamented today. Even a nation handicapped by Labour's rigid controls, could have found the resources to make a comeback in such favourable conditions, drawing on its old tradition in world trade. And in 1951, as if the gods who brood over the capitalist system were smiling upon their old favourite Britain once again, the Tories were returned to power for nearly fourteen years, pledged to achieve this comeback by replacing socialist controls with "freedom"."

They did not achieve it. What went wrong? Two things in particular.

While the main nations of the European mainland began to draw together, first in a coal and steel plan, later in a common market, these early "European" stirrings met with disdain among Tory and Labour leaders alike. Repeated invitations to join were rejected coldly. All these countries had been defeated or occupied during the war, had they not? A superior nation like "victorious" Britain had quite another destiny.

That destiny was to "lead the Commonwealth". Britain was busily dismantling its colonial Empire, and this new-found "family of free nations" would provide rich opportunities in post-war trade. In the Tory phrase of the time, "the Commonwealth comes first in our hearts and in our minds". Dazzled by this mirage, intoxicated by their own speeches, Tory politicians failed to understand how much their country's position had been changed by the war.

A second reason for failure was that the Tories attempted to make their trade comeback with a sadly outdated economy. A century before, while the British Empire was expanding, British predominance had been assured because this country was "the workshop of the world" and the City of London was the centre of its finance. The attempt to repeat history was doomed when New York began to challenge London as the world's financial hub, and in the Far East and elsewhere in the world there were several "workshops" potentially more powerful than Britain's. Nor were the Tory leaders in favour of modernising the outdated British economy. The "free play of market forces" would, they believed, take care of this in good time.

Yet while this rosy dream enthralled politicians in London, the hard fact was that even in the Commonwealth markets soon began slipping from Britain's grasp. Dynamic changes stemming from the immense political and military results of the war began to be felt in economic changes. In the important Australian and New Zealand markets, trade was lost to the United States and Japan, the rising economic powers in (he Pacific area. When China fell to Mao-Tse-tung in 1949 and communist aggression led to a war in Korea in 1950, economic shock waves spread across the world. The recovery of Japan's economy from wartime devastation, already helped greatly by American aid, was further boosted by United States military expenditure in Japan during the Korean War.

Mutual defence was supposed to be one of the bonds uniting the Commonwealth, but after the United States signed a peace treaty with Japan in September 1951, she undertook the defence of Australia and New Zealand under the ANZUS treaty. Britain's declining military power was rubbed in brutally: she was excluded from the ANZUS Pact by all three participants.

Economic repercussions soon followed. From supplying the anti-communist armies in Korea, Japan was well placed to launch further economic drives. The United States did its best to sponsor the overseas trade of its new Pacific protégé. By the mid-1950s sufficient "pull" had been brought to bear on Australia and New Zealand to induce them to give Japan a "most favoured nation" status in their domestic markets. All this, naturally, led to a decline in Britain's exports to the former Dominions.

Britain also lost out in another important Dominion, Canada, but for different reasons. The Ottawa Imperial Preference Agreement of 1932 provided for duty-free imports of Dominion goods into Britain, and a 10 per cent, duty on foreign timber, canned foods, lead, etc. The Dominions imposed duties on manufactured products from countries outside the Empire. Canada's involvement with its big neighbour to the south was greatly increased when war broke out in 1939. The wartime development of Canadian agriculture and industries meant fewer post-war opportunities for Britain. Canada and its immense mineral wealth was included in President Roosevelt's "great arsenal for democracy". After the war, huge United States investments were made in Canada, and that country in turn found the large adjacent American consumer market far more attractive for its wheat, wood, newsprint, paper, minerals and fish, than Britain's.

Another decline of Britain's overseas trade took place in South Africa, though for different reasons again. Though one of our very best markets for some years after the war, it was gradually alienated by the rising tide of anti-apartheid propaganda in this country - another of the direct political results of the war - culminating in Harold Macmillan's "wind of change" speech in 1960. The following year, South Africa withdrew from a hostile Commonwealth. The decline of Britain's once-leading position in the South African market followed swiftly. Today that country buys as much from the United States and Germany as from Britain and it sells most of its mineral wealth to Japan and other Asian industrial countries.

Thus the glowing dream of a great trade future in the Commonwealth crumbled even as Tory speeches extolling it resounded in Westminster. This eclipse of British trade prospects and performance in the precise areas of the world where Tory hopes were highest did nothing to help our obsolescent industries. In 1952, when warning against "the return of the 1930s, only worse", Mosley put his finger on Britain's main economic problem: "The old system has failed. It is a century out of date. In addition the parties have knocked the old machine to pieces by fighting an unnecessary war."

In the post-1945 period, Britain's economy had three main defects. Firstly, with every "go" signalled by an optimistic Chancellor, inflation returned, until a "stop" had to be imposed. Secondly,

Britain was being forced out of her traditional markets by far more efficient rivals like the United States, Germany and Japan. Thirdly, Britain was carrying overseas defence burdens out of all proportion to her economic strength, partly due to her nominal position as "leader of the Commonwealth" and partly in response to the Soviet Communist menace loosed on the world by the war.

One of the ironies of the 1950s and 1960s was that of a Britain maintaining an expensive "East of Suez" military presence in defence of newly-independent Asian countries who showed their gratitude by trading more with Japan than with their protector! This heavy military burden was another direct consequence of the war. Defence of Asian Commonwealth countries whose leaders constantly criticised Britain was what might be called our "eastern" military legacy from the war. There was also a "western" military legacy. Long before Britain condescended to enter the European Community it was committed to help defend Germany under the NATO treaty against Soviet attack. This double defence burden - double what it should have been - added further strains to our creaking economy, which brought about continual balance-of-payments crises.

Such were the years, the inglorious years, when Oswald Mosley's 1930 warning of "a long, slow crumbling" for Britain came true. Even before that lamented "golden age" of expanding world trade had contracted into a world slump, the Tories had muddled Britain's opportunities away. Forced at last to recognise that the United States, Germany and Japan had captured Britain's former best markets, they reluctantly turned to the European Community they had for so long despised.

If ever a man was vindicated by the follies of his opponents in political office, it was Mosley, the "man beyond the pale", the economic heretic whose warnings have been proved true to the very hilt. Towards the end of his life he could say that the real argument about whether he was right or wrong was over. His enemies in their stupendous folly had proved his whole case.

Mosley's Enduring Ideas

"Mosley had a remarkable gift for being in tune with the main historical tendencies of his age. "When his responses to twentieth century challenges are set side by side with those of Britain's rulers, it is their lack of attunement to the new age that appears so striking . . . the very quality of futurism which helped bring his political ambitions to dust keeps his ideas fresh for present and succeeding generations." - Professor Robert Skidelsky

"Mosley, perhaps the most intelligent and rational of all fascist leaders ..." - The Encyclopaedia Britannica

"Mosley's genius soared and fell like a rocket for the saddest of reasons: he was in his ideas a generation too early ... his economic ideas are now almost universally accepted." - Blackwood's Magazine

During his years of wartime imprisonment, Mosley devoted himself to the study of philosophy, from the Greeks to Hegel to Spengler and beyond, with the same concentration that he had given to his study of economics in the 1920s under the guidance of Keynes, and perhaps also of J. A. Hobson. Later, these philosophical studies resulted in a spiritual dimension to his ideas.

After 1945, he devoted himself to updating and streamlining his political and economic policies to meet the entirely new situation of Britain and Europe. He decided that the main objectives of the Corporate State - industrial harmony and a voice for industry in Government - his advocacy of which had in the 1930s brought him many supporters ranging from guild socialists and syndicalists to right-wing Catholics - could be secured by means much simpler than replacement of the existing geographical franchise by an occupational one. An advisory elite of educationists, scientists, industrialists and trade union leaders reporting to the Prime Minister's central administration, together with Government control of incomes through the "wage-price mechanism" would achieve much the same purpose.

Such direct determination of incomes by the Government within an economy largely insulated from the world costing system and the fluctuations of external market prices would have important consequences in dealing with a future problem that he clearly foresaw. Because automation must gradually reduce employment opportunities, the wages system would eventually become an inadequate means of equating consumption with production. The State would then have to provide purchasing power directly to everyone who had been displaced by the machine.

Self-sufficient blocs

Mosley's most far-reaching concept was of a world divided into self-sufficient blocs. Before 1939, the British Empire would have constituted one such bloc. In the immediate post-1945 circumstances he suggested three such spheres of influence: North and South America, Europe and Africa, Russia and Asia. The Soviet Union and its satraps would have to abandon their aim of world communism and genuinely accept the policy to which they constantly pay lip-service: Peaceful Co-existence.

Such an agreed division of the world is the only alternative to a disastrous nuclear conflict. In this New World there would no longer be the intense economic rivalry between nations that led to the First Great War, and a "live and let live" policy would prevent political destabilising in someone's else's sphere.

Europe a Nation

So far, fear of losing their individual cultures and traditions has prevented the nations of Europe from uniting politically as "Europe a Nation'. But the truth is that only the power of Europe united politically as well as economically can protect our national civilisations. Europe must have equality of strength with the two Superpowers, and this necessarily includes military strength.

Defence

Just as Mosley believed that Britain should only fight in self-defence in the 1930s, so he believed that we should only fight in defence of Europe, its overseas territories and vital communications, the Dominions, our vital interests in Africa, and America if attacked in its own territory.

Population

In 1871, the population of the United Kingdom was 27 million. A hundred years later it had grown to over 55 million. Mosley warned that there was an optimum population that Britain could support at a decent standard of living, beyond which the Malthusian argument would rapidly come into effect risking not merely widespread deprivation but actual starvation.

To allow in addition to natural growth, the influx of millions of unassimilable coloured peoples into these small, already crowded islands was madness. It could only lead to the destabilisation of English society and the danger of bloody sectarian conflicts within immigrant communities whose antipathies were centuries old.

Central Government

The machinery of government should be operated directly under the Prime Minister and the Head of the Civil Service and served by a research and economic advisory department together with an executive machine composed of twelve higher officials, probably from the Treasury. The officials in the Prime Minister's department would be joined in the central administration by outsiders from the business world, universities and trade unions. A consolidated Ministry of Science and Technology would be constituted and linked directly with the Prime Minister's department. Thus the scientific revolution would be carried into effect by a continual dynamic drive of government.

In the mid-1970s, Mosley advocated a government of national union, elected for a definite period (say four years) to solve national problems by means of "hard centre" policies, after which it should go to the country to be re-elected or dismissed. This National Government would rule through an Enabling Act and Orders-in-Council, while always remaining liable to dismissal by a vote of censure in Parliament. This government, drawn from the whole nation, would be a "government of experts" - a new-style national government, not an old-style party coalition.

The Economic Problem

Mosley pointed out that as it is impossible for every country to have a favourable balance of payments at the same time, one country or another is bound to have a balance of payments crisis during which it is compelled to restrict credit, deflate, and create depression in order to put itself again in surplus on external account.

Our nineteenth century banking system can no longer achieve equilibrium because it was based on poverty economics. Our Age of Plenty makes it possible for industry to be free of bankers' control, in a system designed for producers. Bankers must find a new role in organising the many new enterprises of a scientific producers' system.

Mosley foresaw "the development of almost fully automatic machinery in which relatively few highly skilled men work machines, or even supervise them". Within a very few years of his death, fully-automated factories were functioning and the problem of man's replacement by machine had become a nightmare one.

Taxation

From 1954, Mosley advocated the transfer of taxes from a direct to an indirect system. His argument was that in the days of poverty economics indirect taxation would have meant a shifting of the burden from rich to poor, but that in our much more affluent society, the direct levy falls hardest on the poorest section of the community, and should be replaced by a graduated indirect system in which only food, clothing and housing would be exempt from taxation. This policy has since been gradually adopted by a succession of British governments.

Unemployment and Public Works

Only two methods of maintaining a high level of employment are possible in peacetime - inflation or large-scale public works. Every unemployed man should have the opportunity of working in a public works programme, which should include retraining and redeployment schemes. But our present structure of government is inadequate to mount, in peacetime, the vast public works schemes that will be required to absorb the future unemployed.

Trade Unions

Trade Union membership, which had grown from 1 million in 1892 to over 12 million in 1960, had declined to 9 million by 1984. Although they had greatly helped the condition of their members in their early days, there had always been disagreement as to whether or not their members' best interests would be served by supporting a particular political cause.

Mosley realised that the growing affluence of the working class would contribute to a decline in trade union membership and power. He proposed that they should resume their former role of providing protection for their members against sickness, industrial accidents and unemployment by taking on some of the functions of the Welfare State and thereby reducing State bureaucracy.

The Wage-Price Mechanism

As science increases the means to produce it will be necessary to equate production and consumption by systematically increasing incomes to provide an adequate market. This can only be done by a central economic authority within an economy largely insulated from the fluctuations of external market prices. In such an economically viable community, prices need not be controlled. They could be left to the free play of competition. The wage-price mechanism would maintain a proper balance between wages, salaries, profits and investment, because power to control the first two automatically affects the two latter. In the event of a grave economic crisis arising before Britain becomes fully integrated into a politically united and economically insulated Europe, the government would have to intervene directly in controlling wages, prices, profits, interest and rents, by a variety of means. This however would be a temporary measure. Once a fully united Europe existed, the wage-price Mechanism would operate as a permanent feature of European economic policy.

Marxism and Communism

Mosley was perfectly familiar with Karl Marx's ideas. John Strachey, later to become the leading English Marxist intellectual, had been Mosley's principal lieutenant from 1924 to 1931. Mosley accepted that Marx had produced the first important overview of human society but considered his analysis to be faulty in almost every detail. Even in 1867, when the first volume of Das Kapital was published, the condition of the working class was changing. The Great Reform Bill of 1832 and the Municipal Corporations Act of 1835 had removed political power from the aristocracy and landed gentry and opened the way for working class enfranchisement.

The course of history and the structure of human societies were not determined, as Marx believed, by blind economic forces but by remarkable individuals. To achieve the universally desired end of an economic system that was both efficient and humane required not class warfare but a class unity that would eventually lead to the disappearance of all classes.

Laissez-faire capitalism had proved efficient as far as the production of wealth was concerned, but inefficient in the way this wealth was distributed. Marxist Communism, by ignoring the mainspring of human motivation, had resulted in societies that are both economically inefficient and inhumane. The real division is not between workers and capitalists but between financiers and producers. Co-ownership and co-partnership can provide workers with both a share of ownership and a share of profits. Eventually technology will reduce the part played by money, banking and finance to a point at which wealth is produced and distributed with minimal human intervention.

The Synthesis of Religion and Science

As soon as man is freed from the oppression of primitive needs - as he soon will be - he can turn his attention to creating a higher form of himself on earth. Having reached his present stage of evolution, man can continue to advance to heights beyond our present vision, if the urge of nature and the purpose of life are to be fulfilled.

The purpose of life is movement from lower to higher forms. This is the way the world works. If we believe in man's destiny we must consciously aid this purpose. Unless man's moral nature and spiritual stature increase commensurately with his material achievements we risk the death of the world. Man must reach beyond his present self, for failure to do this would be final.

Mosley's most enduring gift to posterity is not perhaps his strikingly original ideas on politics and economics but a philosophical and spiritual concept. The man who accepts his doctrine of higher forms, who believes that the purpose of all life is to struggle for the higher, will, in applying this to his own life, discover undreamt-of powers deep within himself. Such a man will find that he can achieve the seemingly impossible; can snatch victory from defeat; and like one of Carlyle's Heroes, give the lie to those who regard man as the helpless victim of blind, impersonal forces.

The Doctrine of Higher Forms derives from the teachings of Heraclitus, that wise old Greek who more than 2,500 years ago summarized in pithy aphorisms all that we are ever likely to know about the meaning of life and the Universe. Mosley acknowledged his debt to him, and would not begrudge him the last word.

All is flux; nothing stays still; nothing remains the same. The opposite is beneficial; from things that differ comes the fairest attunement.

> All things are born through strife
> Nothing endures but change
> Nothing is, but only becomes.

www.ingramcontent.com/pod-product-compliance
Lightning Source LLC
Chambersburg PA
CBHW061753270326
41928CB00011B/2490

* 9 7 8 1 9 1 3 1 7 6 1 4 3 *